IMAGES
of America

DETROIT'S
WOODLAWN CEMETERY

IMAGES
of America

DETROIT'S WOODLAWN CEMETERY

A. Dale Northup

ARCADIA

Published by Arcadia Publishing,
an imprint of Tempus Publishing, Inc.
Charleston SC, Chicago, Portsmouth NH,
San Francisco

Printed in Great Britain.

Library of Congress Catalog Card Number: 2003106972

For all general information contact Arcadia Publishing at:
Telephone 843-853-2070
Fax 843-853-0044
E-Mail sales@arcadiapublishing.com
For customer service and orders:
Toll-Free 1-888-313-2665

Visit us on the internet at http://www.arcadiapublishing.com

CONTENTS

ACKNOWLEDGMENTS

The following individuals and/or organizations were instrumental in making this book become a reality: Einar Kvaran, Dixon, Arizona; Meadowbrook Hall, Oakland University; Roberta Weaver, Woodlawn Cemetery; Karen Jania, Reference Librarian, Lianne Hartman, Student Assistant, Bentley Historical Library, University of Michigan; Larry Raymond, Albert Kahn Associates; Burton Historical Collection, Clarence Burton; Thomas Featherstone, Audio Visual Archivist, Walter P. Reuther Library, Wayne State University; Michael Seneca, Research Coordinator, The Athenaeum of Philadelphia; Donald G. Williamson, Director, McGregor Fund; Patrick DeVinney, Lloyd Brothers Walker Monument Company.

Dedicated to:

Helen Graves Northup and Patricia J. Schneider

INTRODUCTION

The city of Detroit has a rich cultural-industrial history. Its architectural history, however, has been diminished as many significant buildings have been demolished in the path of progress. On the other hand, those which are architecturally imperishable are the magnificent mausoleums and monuments that dot the Detroit cemeteries, most notably at Woodlawn. They are considered among the grandest and noblest architectural works. They are monuments of stone that endure for all time, and upon which the names of the deceased are displayed.

Most of the names on the mausoleums and/or monuments represent individuals who contributed significantly to the architectural, cultural, economic, and social vitality of Detroit. Woodlawn is a time capsule of Detroit history, and can be thought of, paradoxically, as "living history." The cemetery is a tangible link with the past—a repository of community memory.

The mausoleums at Woodlawn represent a microcosm of revival architecture styles: Greek, Roman, and Egyptian. They reflect an homage to past civilizations. The Greek Revival style has been interpreted as a representation of the virtuous citizen who was devoted to public service (of which Woodlawn has many). The Roman Revival style is a re-adaptation of the Greek motif. The Egyptian Revival style draws upon the exotic element of the 19th century which was brought forth with the Napoleonic expeditions to Egypt. Egyptian architecture was admired for its simplicity, solidity, and grandeur. Above all, it had a sense of permanence. With these styles there is an association with greatness. They visually testify to the successful lives of those departed who vied with each other to show off their tastes and their fortunes, lavishing as much on their grave sites as their mansions.

The word mausoleum is derived from a Mausolus, King of Caria, in southwest Turkey. Upon his death in the 4th century B.C., his wife built a magnificent sepulchral monument for his interment in Halicarnassus. The structure was surrounded by 36 monumental Ionic columns on a high base, and it was considered one of the Seven Wonders of the World.

On a similar but smaller scale, the mausoleums at Woodlawn are also magnificent above-ground structures. They are constructed of granite to withstand the elements for centuries to come. They are immune to staining, abrasion, or other damage. Non-corrosive stainless steel dowels and anchors secure the structures.

They were created by artisan hands that link us to the very best of great civilizations that preceded us. Revival styles sought to interpret the best of architectural formulas that tied in with philosophical ideas which have withstood the test of time. From the late 19th to the early 20th centuries, the monument industry thrived in America. For example, many of the mausoleums at Woodlawn were built by the Lloyd Brothers Monument Company, one of the oldest companies in Toledo, Ohio, which also maintained an office in Detroit. The Lloyd business began with Edward Lloyd who left his native Wales as a stonemason and set up shop in Maumee, Ohio. He then passed on the business to his son, John, who was joined by his brother, Edward Jr. The brothers then moved the company to Toledo, Ohio, where they built public and private memorials for every state east of the Mississippi. Harold Willhauck was the chief designer for the Lloyds, having worked 60 years for the company. They hired him right out of high school, where he had completed four years of mechanical drawing courses. The mausoleums and/or monuments at Woodlawn can be viewed collectively as an outdoor museum, taking into consideration the very best and most beautiful of the architecture of past civilizations.

The 140-acre site at Woodlawn was incorporated in 1895 and opened in 1896. It was developed by horticulturalist Frank Eurich, who also developed Woodlawn Cemetery in Toledo, Ohio, and civil engineer Mason L. Brown. Eurich was the co-founder of the Association of American Cemetery Superintendents, formed in 1887. As Detroit grew denser, urbanites sought new burial grounds outside the city. Woodlawn was in fact outside of Detroit city limits the year it was formed. It has been termed a lawn-park cemetery, combining the lawn with the artistry of the mausoleums and monuments. Winding roads, surrounded by mature trees, create a park-like setting. Woodlawn, along with other cemeteries, is considered to be the precursor of what are now known as public parks. This idyllic setting compliments the humanity which rests within it. When the cemetery had an official opening in 1898, board of trustee member Sullivan Cutcheon said, "...we seek a retired spot...for the last resting place of our friends." Confirming that thought is the word cemetery, which means "place of rest."

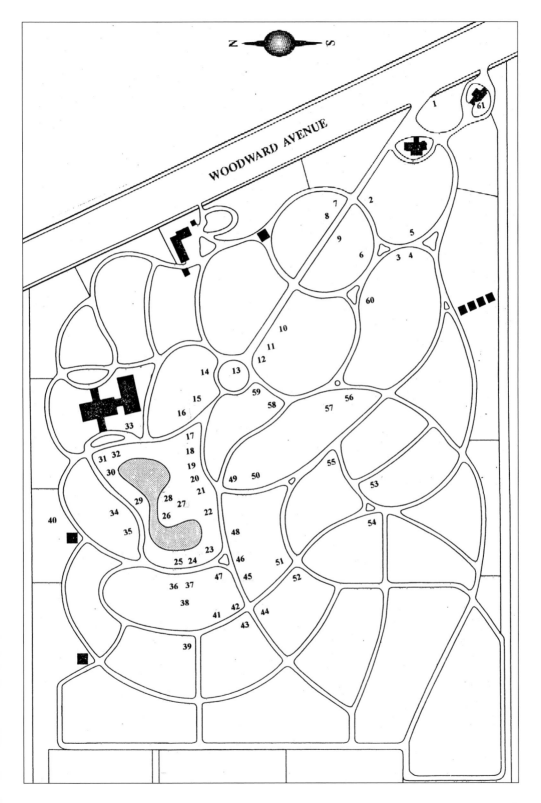

WOODWARD AVENUE

N S

9

One
ENTRANCE,
SECTIONS 3, 4, 5, AND 13

(PLOTS 1–13)

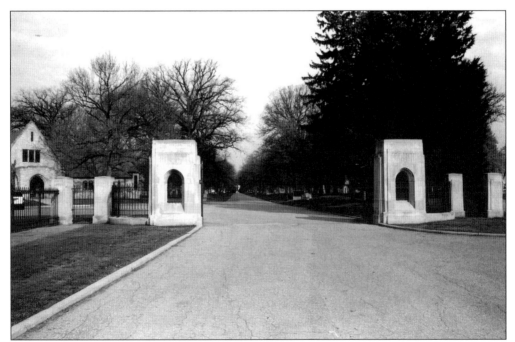

1. ENTRANCE TO WOODLAWN, FRANK EURICH JR., ARCHITECT 1927. Whereas many cemetery entrances are stately, Woodlawn is relatively simple. Openings in the masonry piers suggest a Gothic pointed arch.

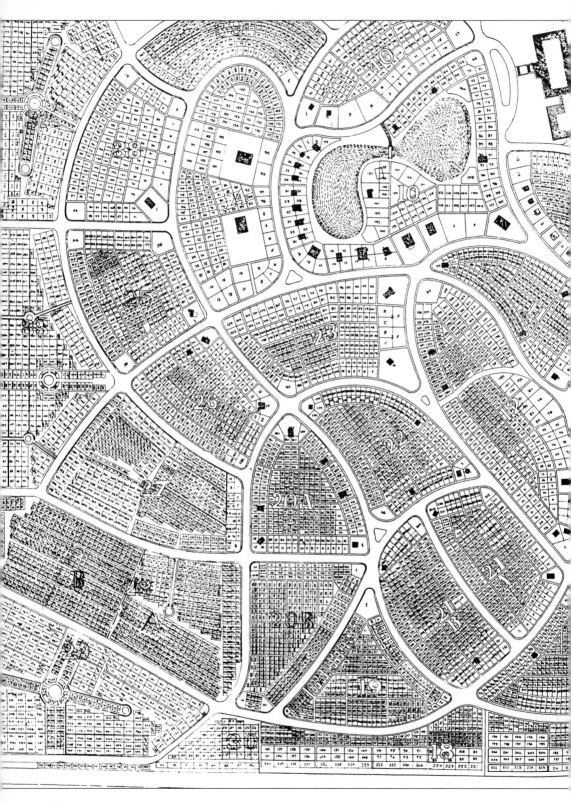

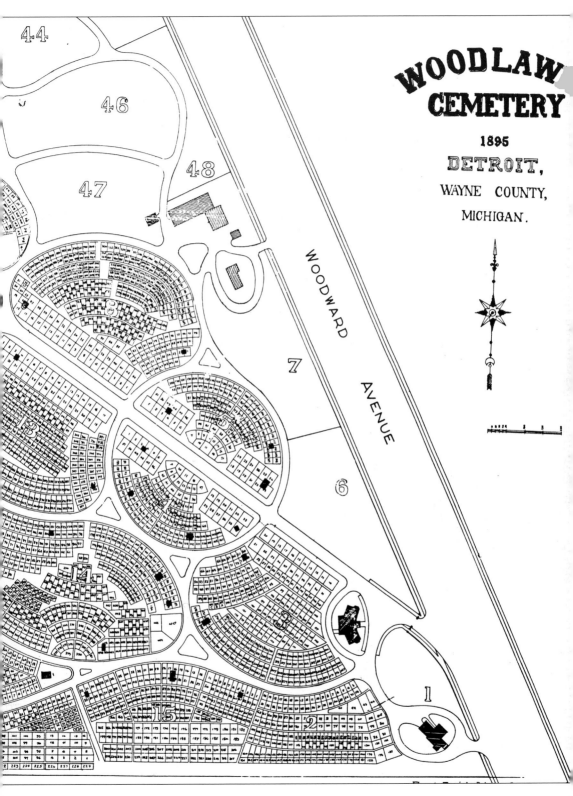

WOODLAW CEMETERY

1895
DETROIT,
WAYNE COUNTY,
MICHIGAN.

WOODWARD AVENUE

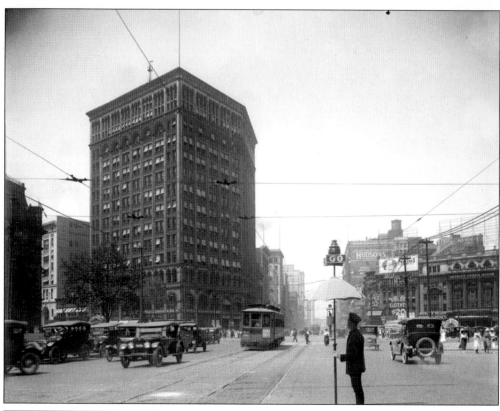

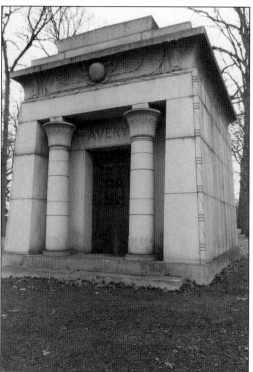

2. WALDO AVERY, 1850–1914. Starting out as a Michigan lumberman based in Saginaw, Avery went on to become the president of the Alabaster Company of Detroit, Chicago, and Alabaster, Michigan. It was incorporated into the U.S. Gypsum Company in 1902. Gypsum, a form of alabaster, was one of the earliest known Michigan minerals. It was the Alabaster Company that furnished the plaster for the staff in the construction of the buildings at the Columbian Exposition in Chicago (1893). Avery was a major investor in Detroit's Majestic Building (1895; demolished 1962). It was designed by Chicago's notable architect Daniel H. Burnham. (Photo courtesy Walter P. Reuther Library, Wayne State University.)

The Avery mausoleum is designed in the Egyptian Revival style. Over the name is a winged sun disk in the concave cornice. It appears on the entrances of many tombs and temples in ancient Egypt and commemorates the victory of light over darkness, along with the life-giving properties of the sun. Cobras are on either side of the sun disk. These can also be seen on the headpieces of ancient pharaohs, serving in a protective capacity. The entrance is flanked by imposing papyrus-capped columns with triangular stalks in the papyrus. Ancient Egypt suggested sturdy, permanent architecture and an impressive tradition of the funerary arts.

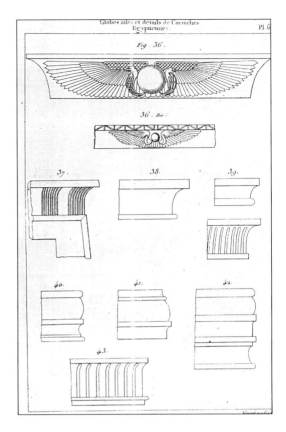

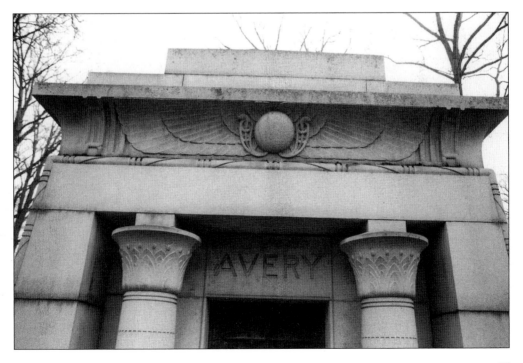

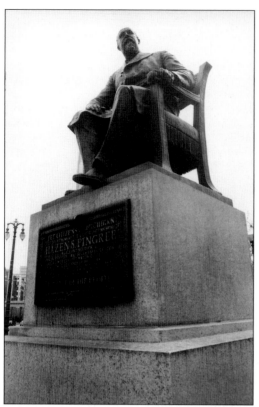

3. HAZEN PINGREE, 1840–1901. Pingree was originally from Massachusetts and fought in the Civil War, during which he was taken prisoner and eventually escaped. After the war, he came to Detroit, where he started out in the shoe business. He helped to make Detroit one of the largest shoe manufacturing centers in the country.

He was the 35th Mayor of Detroit (1890–97) during which time he did much to clean up the corrupt city government. He was re-elected three times. The first time, he was elected as a Republican by a margin of 2300 votes in what was then heavily Democratic Detroit. The third time he received 67 percent of the popular vote. He became the idol of the people and was considered a vigorous defender of the working man. When employees of a streetcar company dumped a trolley into the Detroit River, protesting low wages, Mayor Pingree not only refused to have them thrown in jail, but said he would like to have been part of the mob. Pingree then went on to successfully fight for public ownership of public transportation. The Panic of 1893 put thousands of people out

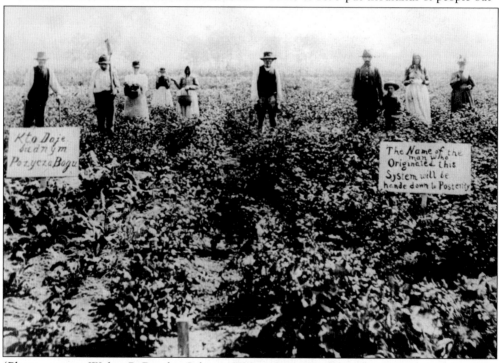

(Photo courtesy Walter P. Reuther Library, Wayne State University.)

of work. Pingree had vacant land in the city plowed up for gardens on which residents could grow their own food. He was twice elected Governor of Michigan (1897–1901), and during his first term he continued to serve as the Mayor of Detroit. The State Supreme Court ruled against it, so Pingree chose the governorship. When he became governor, Pingree threw a party on the floor of the Michigan House of Representatives which was attended by future president Theodore Roosevelt dressed in his Rough Riders cavalry uniform.

As governor, Pingree added millions to the revenue of the State of Michigan by forcing taxation of railway property, and added to the state appropriation for public schools. As governor, he became involved in the Progressive Movement, which was a national campaign for extensive economic, political, and social reform. When Pingree retired after his second term as governor in 1901, he gave a final address to the Legislature: "It is your special privilege and duty to bring the so-called 'merchant princes' and 'captains of industry' in this country to a realization of the fact that our laboring men are something more than tools to be used in the senseless chase after wealth."

The citizens of Michigan were instrumental in erecting a larger than life-size statue of Pingree in downtown Detroit's Grand Circus Park. A plaque on the pedestal lauds him as "The idol of the people." Austrian sculptor Rudolph Schwartz, who immigrated to the United States, won the competition for the statue in 1902.

The Pingree mausoleum is Classical Revival in the Roman style with a portico on the front. The triangular pediment is supported by Corinthian columns favored by the Romans.

The name Sherman Depew, also interred, appears on the mausoleum. Depew was Pingree's son-in-law and treasurer-general manager of Pingree's shoe business. Depew was married to Pingree's daughter Frances, who is also interred with her husband.

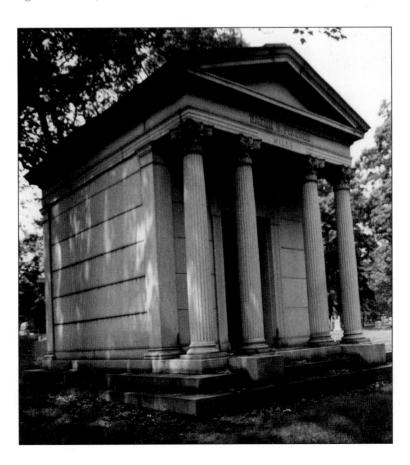

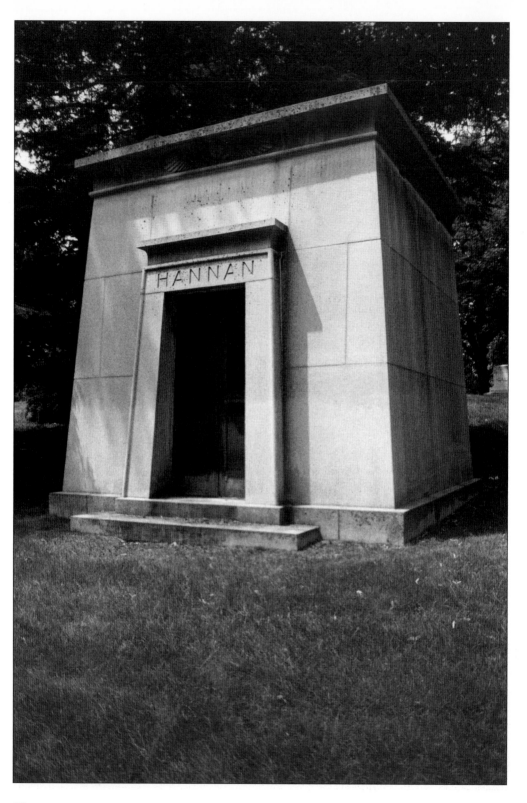

4. WILLIAM W. AND LUELLA HANNAN, 1859–1928. William W. Hannan began in the Detroit real estate business in 1883, forming the Hannan Real Estate Exchange. He was involved in the development of subdivisions in Detroit and the suburbs, as well as the Pasadena, Madison, and Lennox apartment buildings.

In 1925, Luella Hannan founded the Luella Hannan Memorial Foundation to serve aged people in Detroit and the city's tri-county area.

The Hannan mausoleum is a modest Egyptian Revival structure in the form of a mastaba, which is the Arabic word for bench. It's basically a pyramidal structure with the top cut off. A winged disk is over the door. (Photo courtesy Luella Hannan Memorial Foundation.)

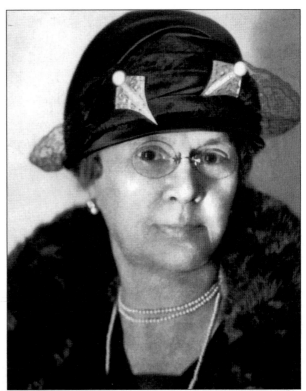

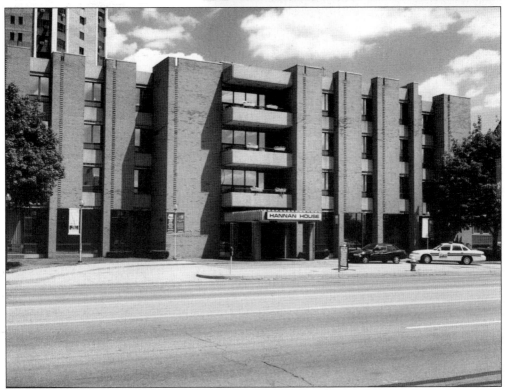

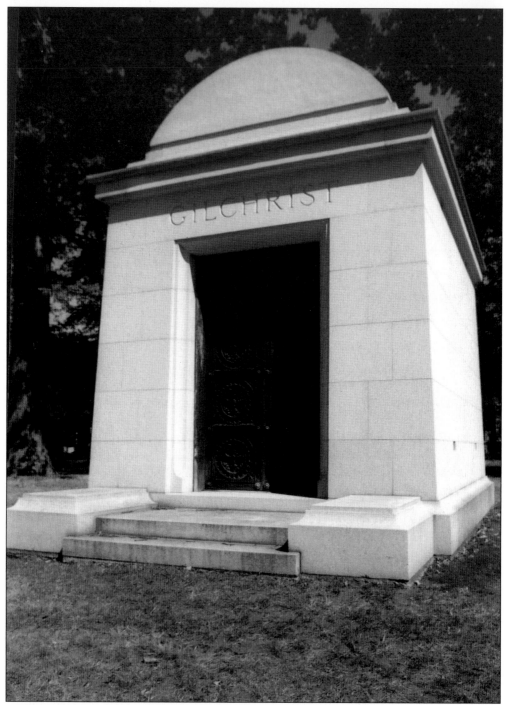

5. FRANK W. GILCHRIST, 1845–1912. Gilchrist founded a transportation company that was involved shipping coal and iron ore on the Great Lakes. Prior to his involvement in the shipping business, Gilchrist was involved with lumbering in the Saginaw area.

The Gilchrist mausoleum is an imposing limestone structure with a vaulted roof. The interior, as with other mausoleums, is lined with marble.

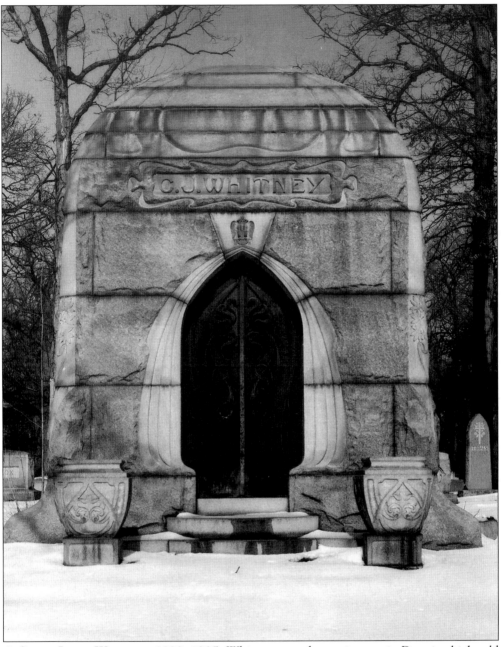

6. CLARK JAMES WHITNEY, 1832–1905. Whitney owned a music store in Detroit which sold pianos and organs. He then went on to own a chain of theaters in Michigan and Ontario, including the Detroit Opera House, of which he was lessee from 1879 until his death. C.J. helped to ensure that the country's most famous performers from grand opera to Shakespeare, vaudeville, and circus, returned to the city year after year. Son Bertram succeeded his father to become President of the Whitney Amusement Company and manager of the Detroit Opera House. He is credited with bringing the first motion picture projection to Michigan in 1896.

C.J. also was one of the first individuals to acknowledge the possibilities of electricity, serving to organize the Brush Electric Company in 1880, which became Detroit Edison in 1902.

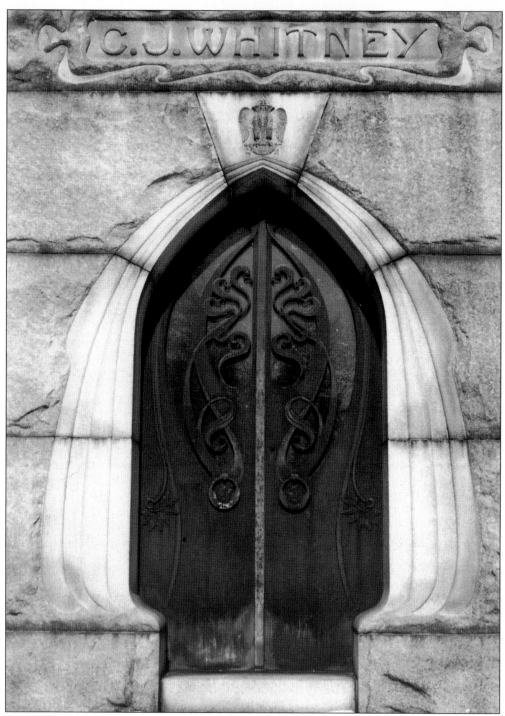

The design of the entrance doors, in this beehive-like tomb, is done in the Art Nouveau style with dramatically swirling plant forms that seem to symbolize the theatricality of Whitney's business ventures. The stonework is roughly hewn with incised joints and sweeping plant forms in relief on the corners of building.

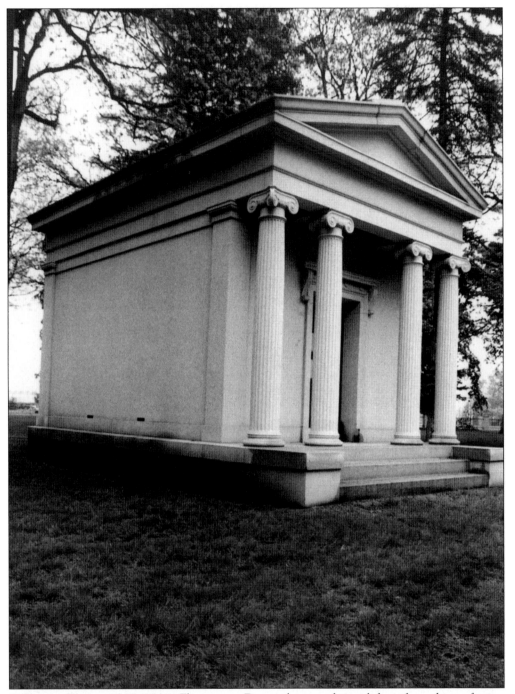

7. ELISHA FLINN, 1843–1911. Flinn was a Detroit lawyer who withdrew from the profession to become involved in the business of buying and selling timber pine. He operated in Michigan, Minnesota, and Wisconsin. He had large tracts of pine acreage in Minnesota upon which iron ore was discovered, and it was leased to mining companies.

The Flinn mausoleum is an imposing Greek Revival Ionic temple-like structure. The door head over the entrance is supported by graceful scroll brackets.

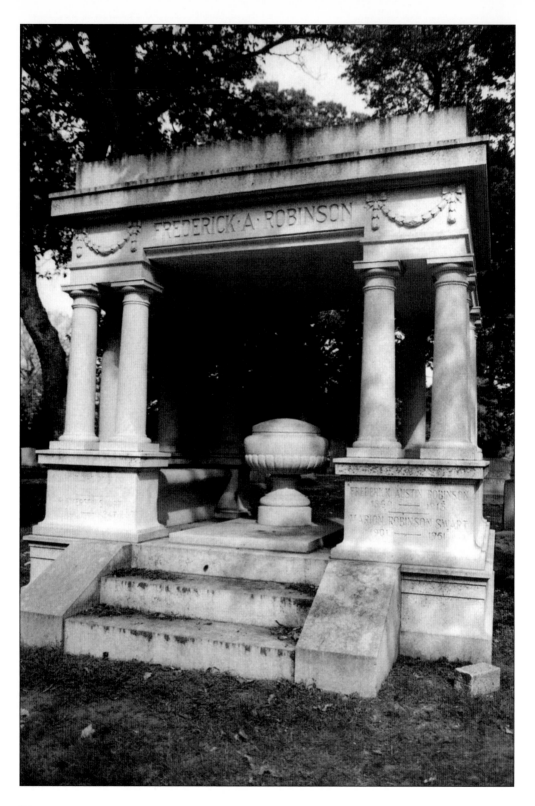

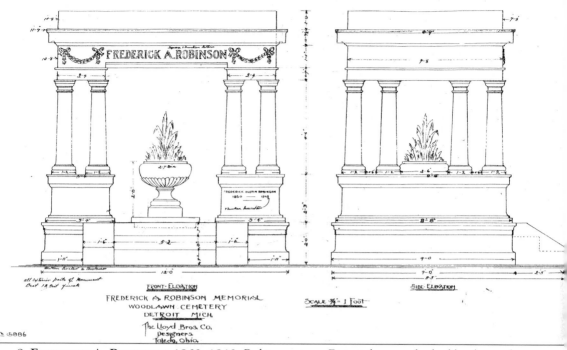

FREDERICK A. ROBINSON MEMORIAL
WOODLAWN CEMETERY
DETROIT MICH.

The Lloyd Bros Co.
Designers
Toledo, Ohio.

8. FREDERICK A. ROBINSON, 1860–1913. Robinson was a Detroit lawyer who had lumber and mining interests in Michigan, Minnesota, and Wisconsin.

This peristyle monument has columns that go all the way around an open interior space which contains an urn that could possibly hold ashes of the deceased. The columns are Tuscan which is a simplified version of the Doric order. They flank an entrance which has been referred to as "the portal of eternity." Above the columns are swags, or festoons, on either side of the Robinson name, used for decoration.

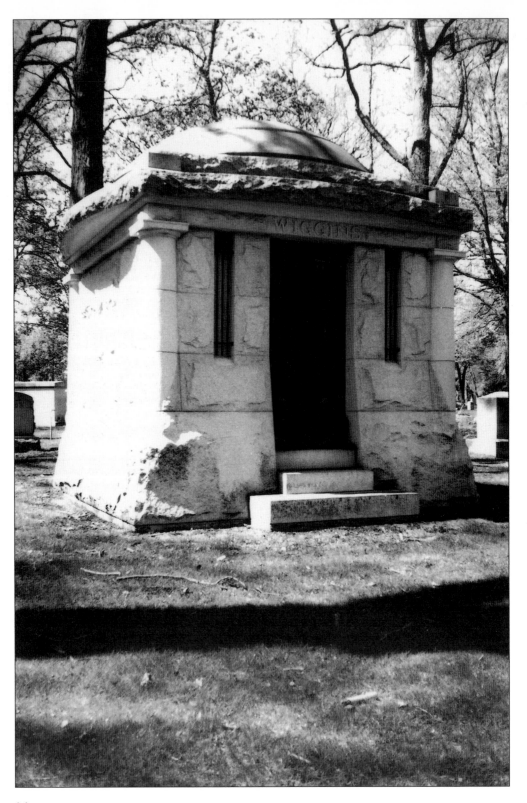

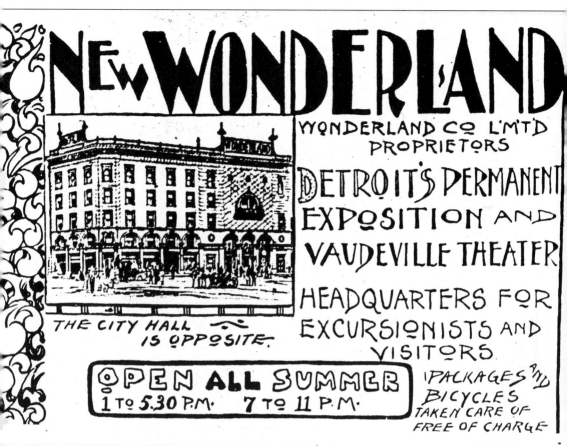

9. ENOCH WIGGINS, 1843–1907. After touring the country with the circus as a young man, Wiggins returned to Detroit. In 1885, he started the Wonderland Theater, whose wax figures and wild animals fascinated children for years. He then closed the Wonderland and devoted all his energies in 1901 to the vaudeville section of the house, which he named the Temple Theater. It was vaudeville with some of the best performers: Jack Benny, Jimmy Durante, and Sophie Tucker. The Temple became the goal of every ambitious vaudevillian. It had the distinction of being one of the best variety houses west of New York. Wiggins was considered the last of the picturesque showmen in Detroit.

The Wiggins mausoleum is an impressive structure with a masonry dome, roughly hewn stonework with a canted base, and Doric columns which flank the four corners.

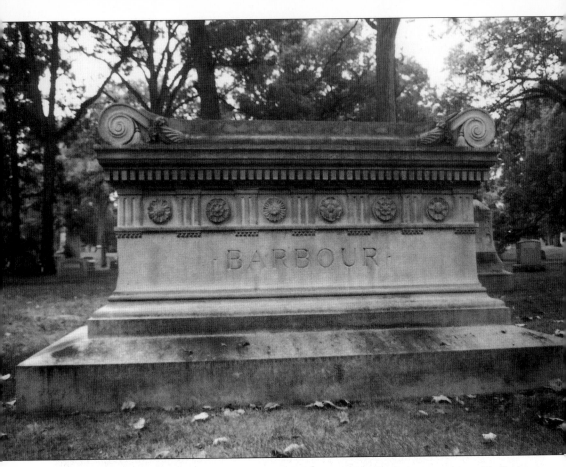

10. LEVI LEWIS BARBOUR, 1840–1925. Barbour was a successful Detroit attorney. To Barbour belongs the title "The father of the park," namely Belle Isle, which he first conceived purchasing. Late in the fall of 1878, he consulted with various citizens on the possibility of a purchase from the Campeau heirs who owned the island. On his own account, Barbour obtained options on portions of the island. Finally a bond issue was passed by the city council, and the island was purchased in 1879. When he died, Barbour left a generous bequest to beautify Belle Isle which resulted in the Barbour fountain (1937). It was designed by notable Michigan sculptor Marshall Fredericks—his first major public commission. A spirited bronze gazelle leaps with its head thrown back. At the base are four figures: rabbit, hawk, otter, and grouse, carved out of black granite. On the rim of the fountain is the inscription that suggests Barbour's motivation: "A continual hint to my fellow citizens to devote themselves to the benefit and pleasure of the public." As another part of his civic involvement, Barbour was appointed to the Library Commission in1881, which was then under the control of the Detroit Board of Education. Barbour was also on the Board of Regents at the University of Michigan (1892–98, 1902–08) of which he was a graduate. In 1920, he built the Betsey Barbour women's dormitory, named after his mother.

The Barbour monument is an exact replica of the Scipio Barbatus (3rd century B.C.) sarcophagus, the earliest known Roman sarcophagus, now in the Vatican Museum. Scipio was a Roman general and consul. This is the most imitated of ancient monuments, suggesting an association with ancient Roman grandeur. The monument is decorated with a band that contains three vertical members (triglyphs) each side of which contains rosettes of varying patterns. Above the band is an Ionic top with spirals at either end.

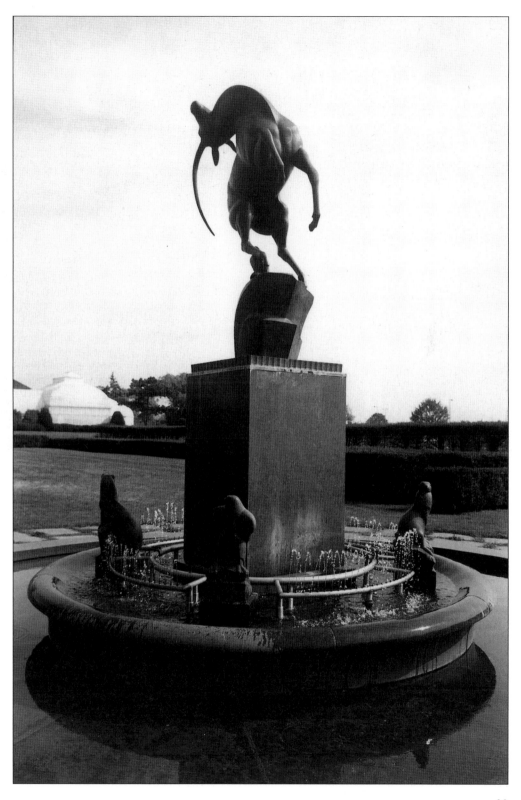

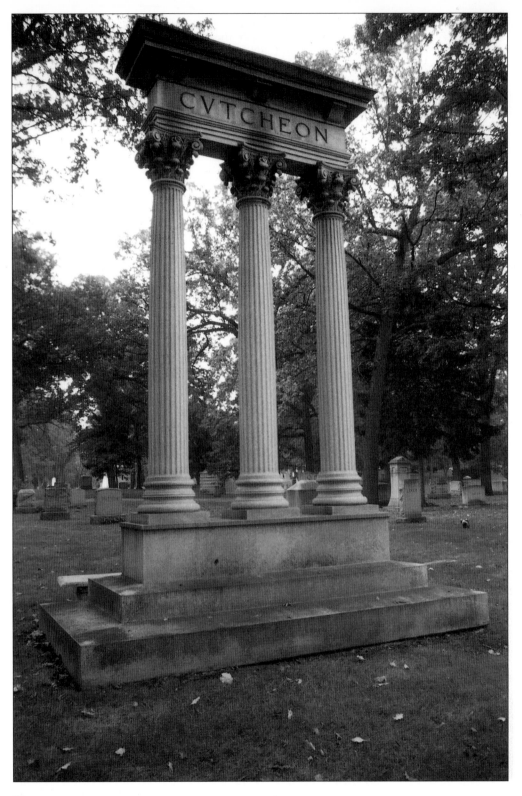

11. SULLIVAN M. CUTCHEON, 1833–1900. A loyal supporter of the Fort Street Presbyterian Church in Detroit, Cutcheon served as an elder there. Second Presbyterian Church was organized in 1849 and renamed Fort Street. Built of limestone in the Gothic Revival style, the building was dedicated in 1855.

Cutcheon was a member of the House of Representatives in the State of Michigan (1861–64), serving as speaker the house (1863–64). In 1884, he was President of the Dime Savings Bank when it was organized. Cutcheon was on the first board of directors of Woodlawn Cemetery in 1895. He was also on the board of trustees of Harper Hospital and instrumental in raising $200,000 for its endowment.

The Cutcheon monument draws upon Roman antiquity with three Corinthian columns. The column attains an important scale of classic beauty without the mass of wall. The Cutcheon name is incised in Roman letters.

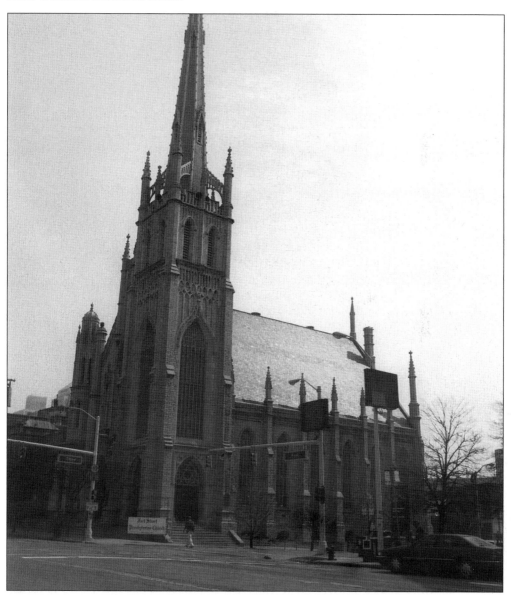

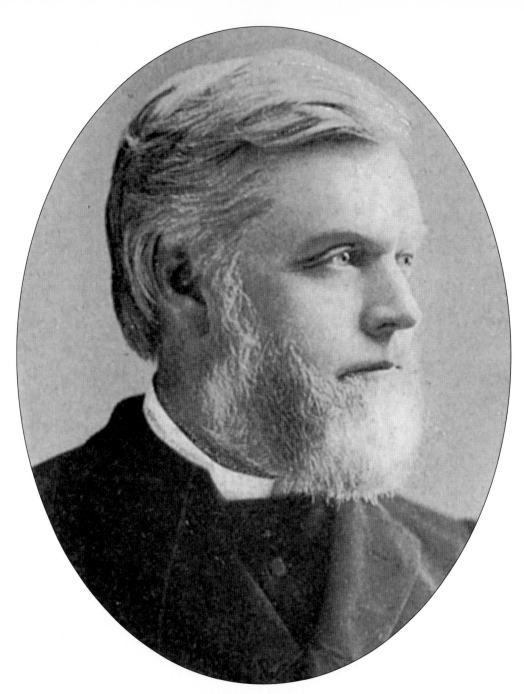

12. William Xavier Ninde, 1832–1901. Ninde was pastor of the Central Methodist Episcopal Church in Detroit (1876–79). He was made a bishop of the Methodist Episcopal Church in 1884. The church was designed by notable Michigan Gothic Revival architect Gordon Lloyd and completed in 1867. At the time of its construction, it was considered the finest Methodist church in Michigan. Now called the Central United Methodist Church, it has been called "the conscience of the city." Pre-empting this, Ninde had an abiding faith in the good work that Christianity could do.

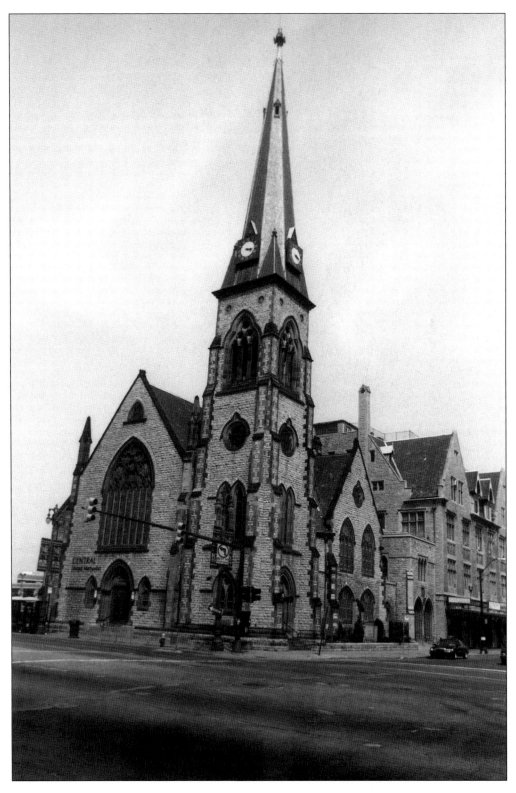

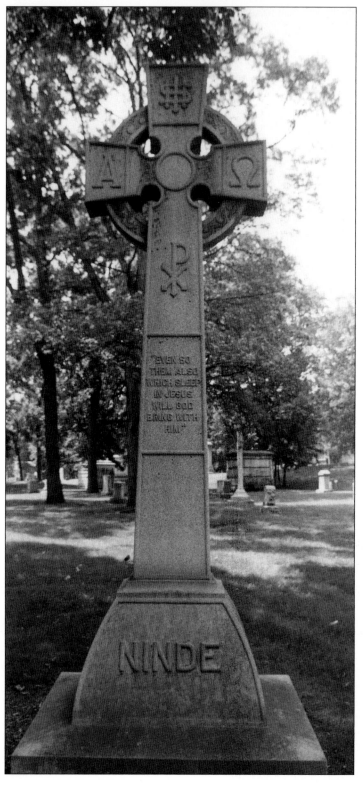

The Ninde plot is marked by a Celtic cross which dates back to the 10th century in Ireland and Scotland. The cross is a Christian symbol that signifies the unity of heaven and earth. The vertical member tapers outward toward the base. At the junction of the vertical and horizontal members, the cross is hollowed out in four places inscribed within a circle that represents timelessness or eternity. Whereas many Celtic crosses are elaborately carved, this one is relatively simple.

The letters X and P, on the vertical member, are the Greek letters for Chi Rho, an abbreviation for the word Christ. This is one of the earliest Christian symbols. On the top of the vertical member, what looks like a dollar sign is actually the letters I, H, and S superimposed. They are an anagram for the Latin words "In hac salus," "in this cross is salvation." The signs on either end of the horizontal member are the Greek letters Alpha and Omega, the first and last letters of the alphabet. They are based on Revelation 1:8, "I am the Alpha and Omega, the beginning and the ending, saith the Lord."

Two
SECTIONS 11, 9, AND 10

(PLOTS 14–33)

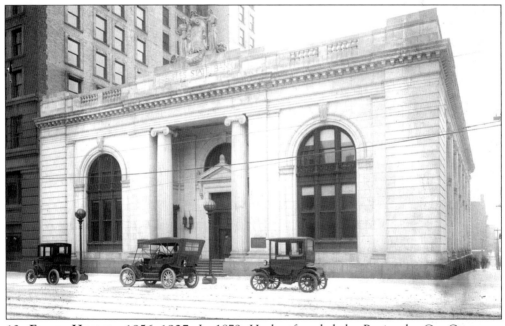

13. FRANK HECKER, 1856–1927. In 1879, Hecker founded the Peninsular Car Company, makers of railroad cars in Detroit. He was also involved in the organization of the Union Trust Company in 1890. Hecker was appointed by President Theodore Roosevelt to the Panama Canal Commission. When Hazen Pingree was Mayor of Detroit in the late 19th century, Hecker came to tell him he wanted to run for Congress. Pingree's reply, being pro-labor, was how he could expect people to vote for him when he paid his workers 90¢ a day. Hecker never had a public career; however, he did serve to organize Woodlawn Cemetery in 1895. As President of the Board of Directors at Woodlawn, Hecker chose a plot at the end of the major thoroughfare leading into the cemetery, making for prominent visibility. (Photo courtesy Walter P. Reuther Library, Wayne State University.)

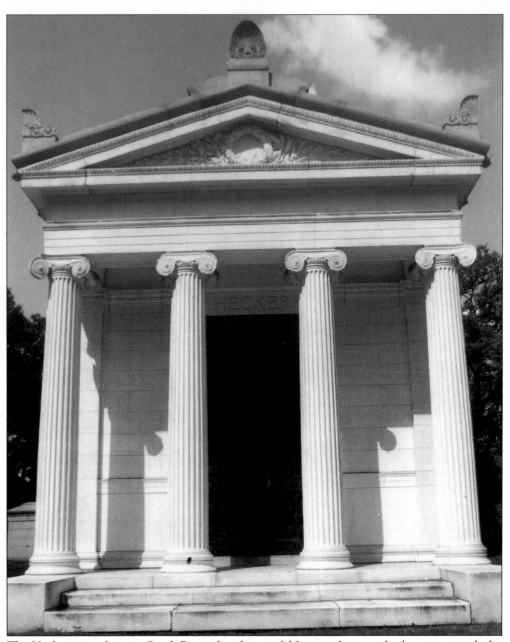

The Hecker mausoleum is Greek Revival with graceful Ionic columns, which contrast with the more austere strength of the Doric order. Acroteria, ornamental projections, mark the three corners of the triangular pediment. It is built of marble, the only mausoleum at Woodlawn made of this material, as the majority are granite. It was designed by Stanford White, of the New York architectural firm McKim, Mead and White, in 1897. White is probably one of the best-known American architects of the late 19th Century. Chares Lang Freer, business partner and neighbor of Hecker, was a friend of White's and arranged a meeting between the two men that lead to the design. The following year the People's State Bank in Detroit, of which Hecker was on the board of directors, also hired the firm to design the bank building in 1898. State Savings Bank became People's State Bank in 1917.

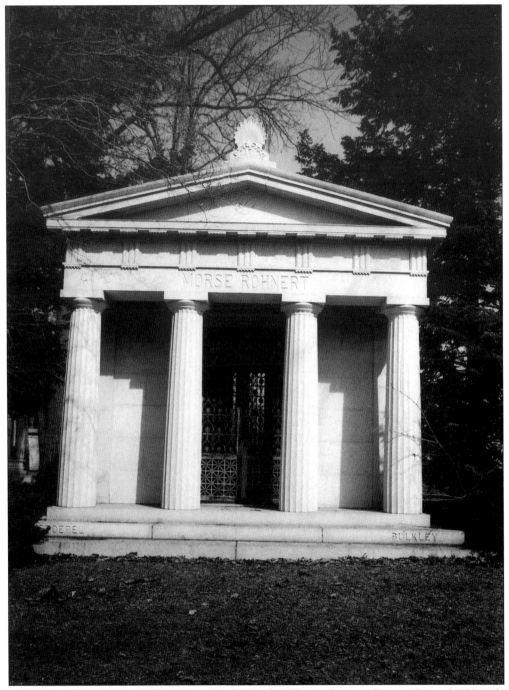

14. MORSE ROHNERT, 1864–1911. A judge in the Wayne County Circuit Court (1900–11), Rohnert was also President of the Michigan Cigar Box Company, along with being the Vice President of the Schober Printing Company in Detroit.

The mausoleum is Greek Revival. Much like a Greek temple, it adheres to the use of triglyphs, three vertical members, spaced evenly on the horizontal band above the Doric Columns. An acroterium ornament is atop the triangular pediment, perhaps signifying leadership.

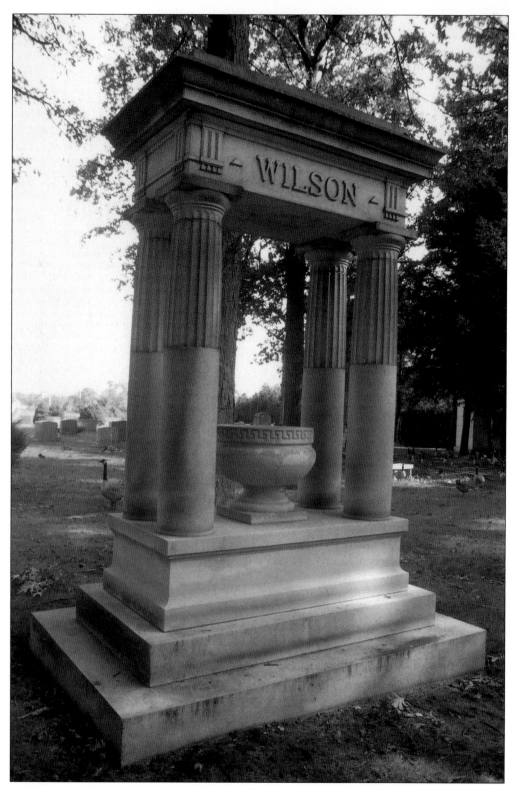

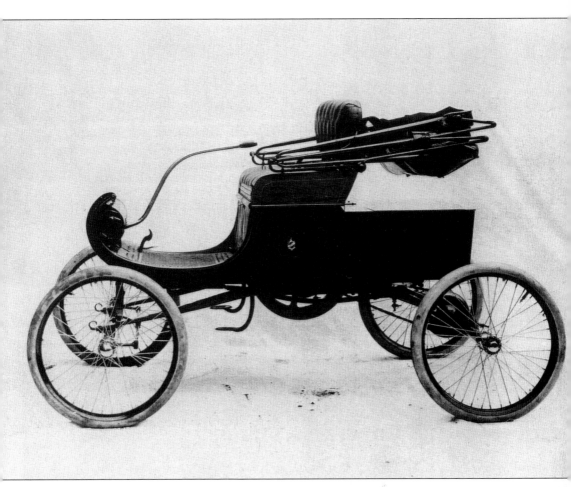

15. CHARLES ROBERT WILSON, 1844–1915. In 1875, Wilson started out as a carriage builder in Detroit. He went on to become a pioneer builder of wooden bodies and cushions, in the day of the curved dash automobile, for three principle auto companies: Ford, Cadillac, and Olds. In 1904, Fred, Edward, and Charles Fisher had their first contact with automobiles as employees of the C.R. Wilson Company, before they went into business for themselves and became part of General Motors. The C.R. Wilson Company merged with three other Detroit body makers in 1924, forming the Murray Corporation of America.

The Wilson monument is classically conceived with triglyphs over the columns and the Greek key pattern on the urn. One interesting feature is the vertical fluting on the columns which goes only halfway down.

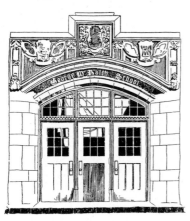

Dedicatory Exercises

George W. Balch School

Auditorium George W. Balch School
Friday, February 24, 1922
9:30 a. m.

16. GEORGE W. BALCH, 1832–1908. Balch was the first president of the Detroit School Board (1873–77) and a member of the Detroit Board of Alderman (city council) in 1878. An elementary school in Detroit bears his name. He is considered the father of the telephone in Michigan. In 1877, he bought a state agency from the Bell enterprises and formed the Telegraph and Telephone Construction Company in Detroit, which then became Michigan Bell in 1878. When telephones were installed, Detroit had one of the first telephone exchanges in the U.S. Telephone customers were assigned phone numbers to facilitate handling calls themselves. Balch was also involved with the incorporation of the Edison Electric Company in 1881.

The Balch mausoleum is Egyptian Revival with simple papyrus plants in relief that border the entrance. The papyrus motif is repeated in the grillwork on the doors.

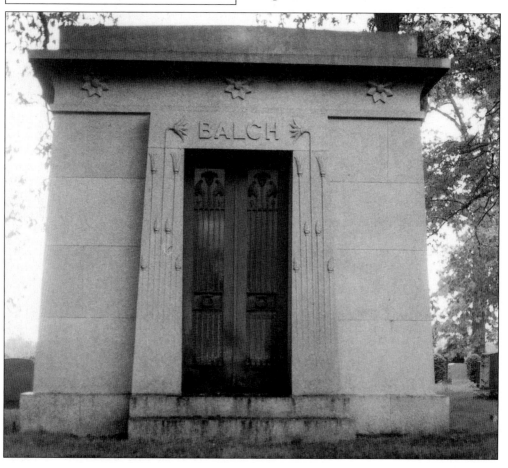

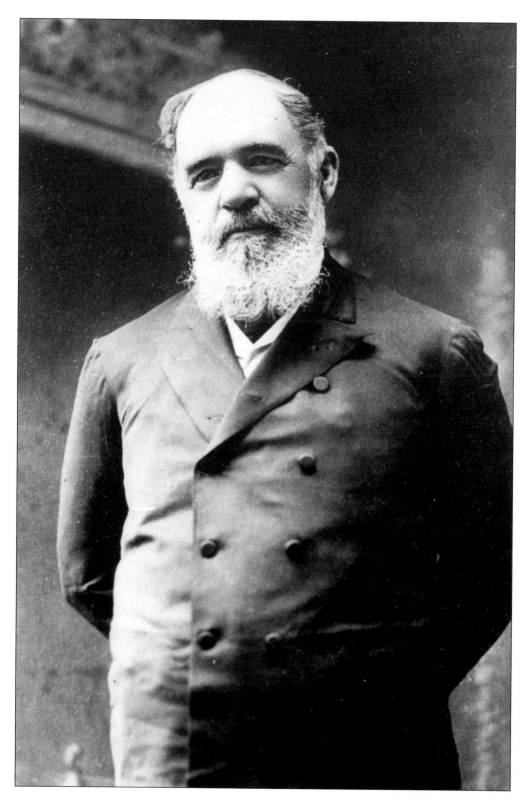

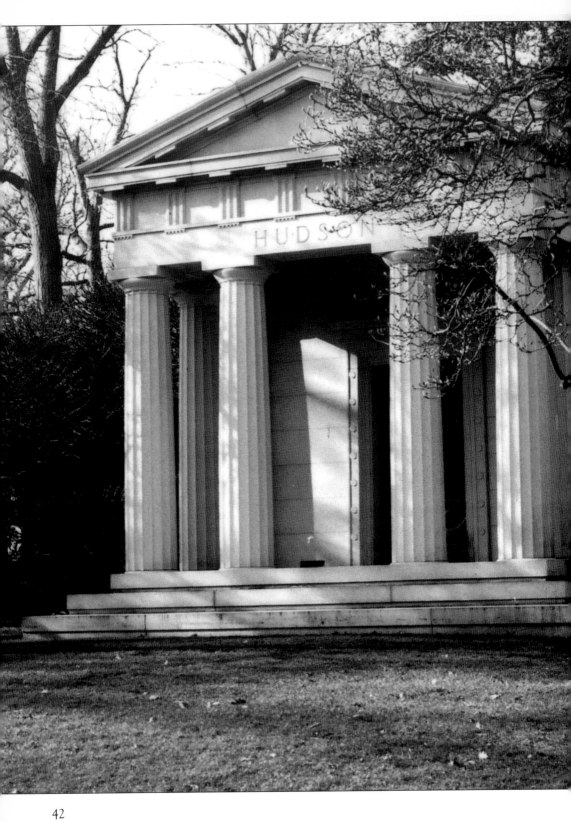

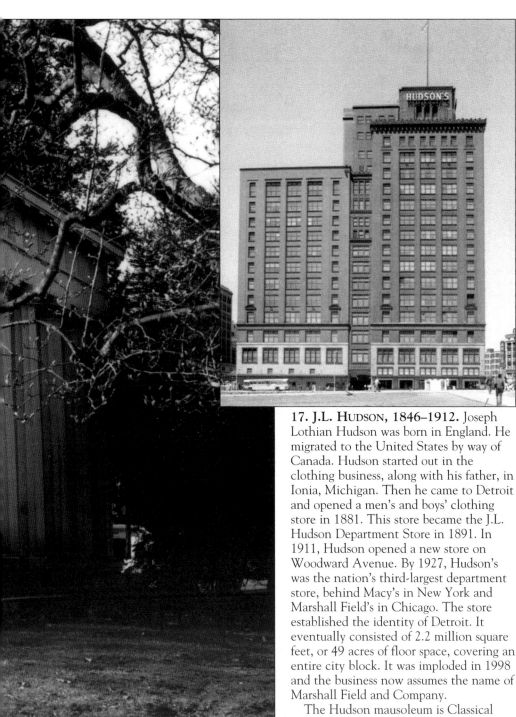

17. J.L. HUDSON, 1846–1912. Joseph Lothian Hudson was born in England. He migrated to the United States by way of Canada. Hudson started out in the clothing business, along with his father, in Ionia, Michigan. Then he came to Detroit and opened a men's and boys' clothing store in 1881. This store became the J.L. Hudson Department Store in 1891. In 1911, Hudson opened a new store on Woodward Avenue. By 1927, Hudson's was the nation's third-largest department store, behind Macy's in New York and Marshall Field's in Chicago. The store established the identity of Detroit. It eventually consisted of 2.2 million square feet, or 49 acres of floor space, covering an entire city block. It was imploded in 1998 and the business now assumes the name of Marshall Field and Company.

The Hudson mausoleum is Classical Revival in the Roman style with a portico on the front and engaged columns on the side that are attached to the walls. (Photo courtesy Walter P. Reuther Library, Wayne State University.)

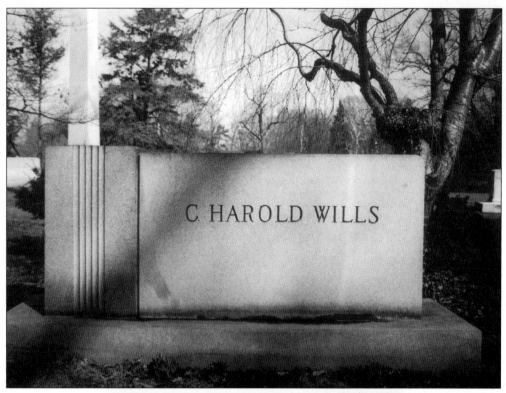

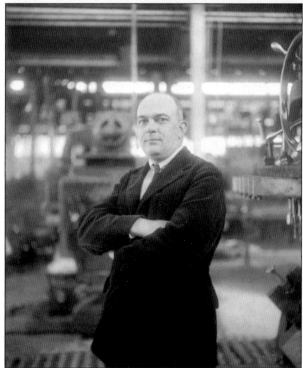

(Photo courtesy Walter P. Reuther Library, Wayne State University.)

18. CHILDE HAROLD WILLS, 1879–1941. Wills was the son of a master mechanic in Fort Wayne, Indiana, whose talents he inherited. He served apprenticeships in machine shops while he read technical journals and worked over his drafting board. His mechanical genius was recognized at an early age. He became a machinist at age 17 and went on to become an expert machinist three years later. His first significant appointment was with the Boyer Machine Company as an engineer. Then he went on to work for Henry Ford from 1903 through 1919. Wills was considered Ford's mechanical catalyst. Ford was often quoted as saying that, without Wills, the Model T never could have been the success that it was. He could fashion one feature after another of the automobile from Ford's crude pencil sketches. The metallurgy that Wills put into the development of the car was vanadium steel that was one reason why it was so indestructible. He refined the metal manufacturing process until it could be produced in large enough quantities to satisfy the low-priced Fords.

Ford bought out Wills in 1919 for $1.5 million. Wills then went on to create his own car - the Wills St. Claire which became a state-of-the art automobile. Wills produced 14,000 cars at his Marysville plant (1921-26). Unfortunately, Wills' mechanical exactitude, along with the high cost of the car, got in the way in the way of its successful production which was retired in 1926.

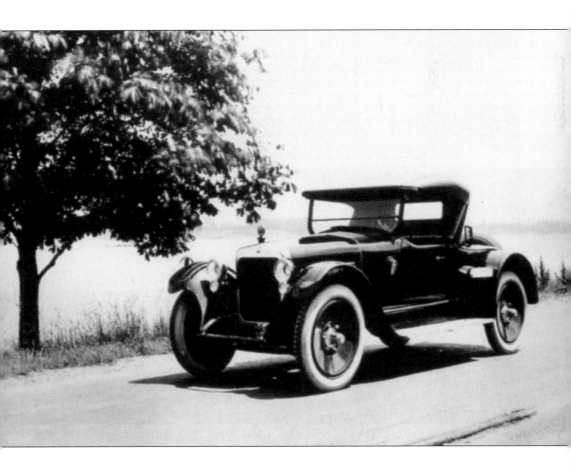

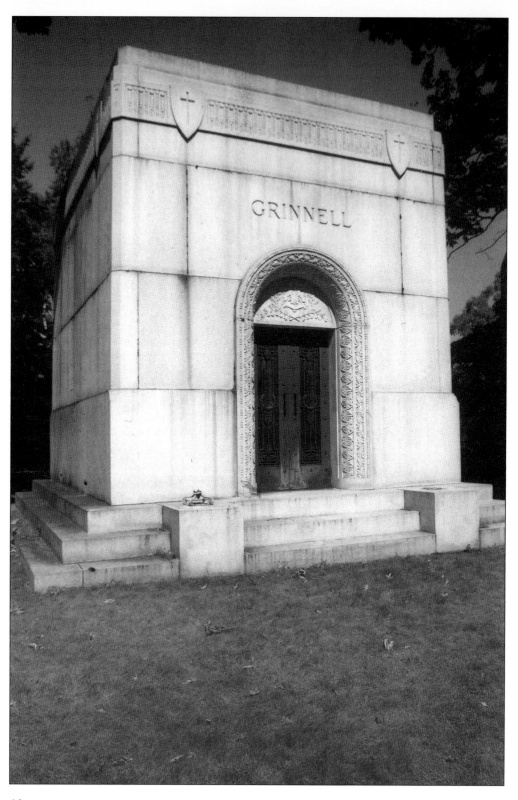

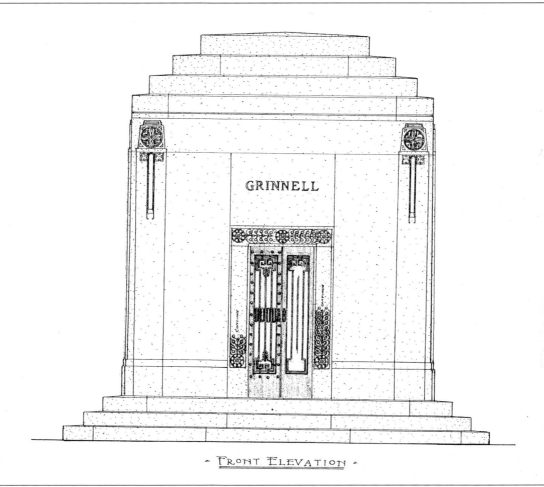

GRINNELL

- FRONT ELEVATION -

19. CLAYTON GRINNELL, 1860–1927. Grinnell moved with his brother, Ira, from Ann Arbor to Detroit in 1882. Upon their arrival, they started out in the sewing machine business. They then established a music business selling pianos, organs, and other musical merchandise. Clayton and Ira began manufacturing pianos in 1901. Grinnell's became the largest business of its kind in the country, with twenty branch stores in Michigan, as well as Canada.

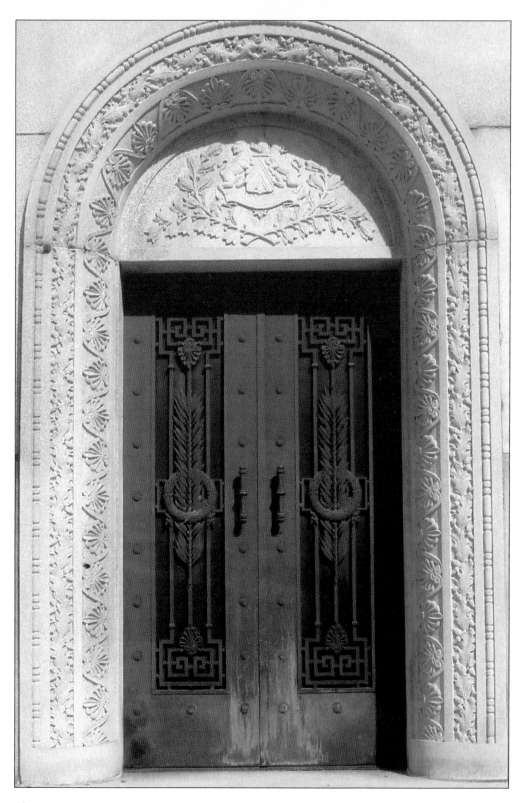

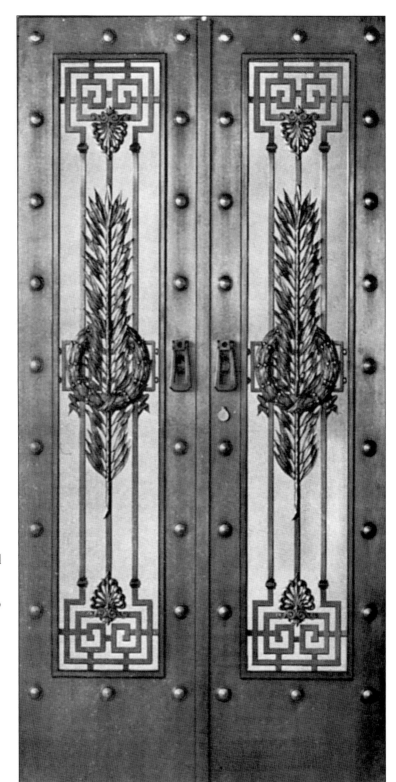

The Grinnell mausoleum is a substantial limestone building created by the Lloyd brothers of Toledo, Ohio. The original plan was changed to include an arched entry with the family coat of arms, which was used on the store plate, under the arch. An elaborate floral-leaf motif lines the doorway. The doors were done by the Detroit Mausoleum Equipment Works.

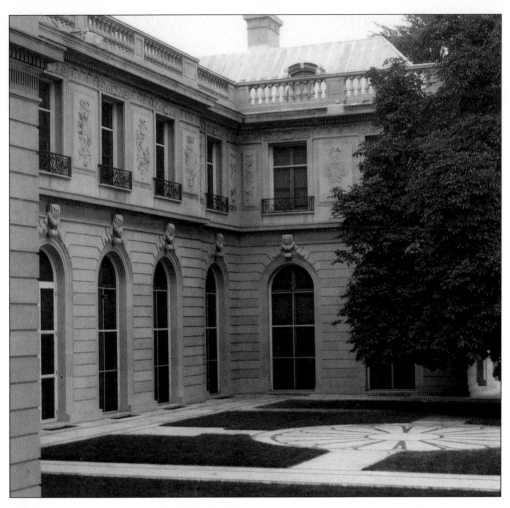

20. JOHN AND HORACE DODGE, 1864–1920, 1868–1920. In 1901, John and Horace Dodge opened a machine shop in Detroit that became one the largest parts-manufacturing firms in the U.S. They were admired for their ability to produce excellent machine work. Their first contract in the auto business was to produce transmissions for the original Oldsmobile runabout. They were then hired by Henry Ford, in 1903, to build motors, transmissions, and steering gear for the first Ford cars. John and Horace became owners of 20 percent of the entire stock of Ford Motor Company. They began to produce their own automobile in 1913, which annoyed Ford, since they were using the dividends from Ford stock they owned to start their own company. Like Ford, the Dodge brothers emphasized the production of one type of car without departing from the original design. They were pioneers in the construction of all-steel bodies. The Dodge automobile achieved a reputation for "dependability" because buyers praised the car's power and rugged construction.

John and Horace have been described as fighters, but, had they not been, they would never have accomplished what they did. They are considered legendary figures in the early auto industry. From the beginning, John handled all the business dealings, whereas Horace handled most of the mechanical innovations. When decisions had to be made, neither one acted without the approval of the other. When John died in 1920, Horace never recovered from the shock of his brother's death. He lost interest in the vast manufacturing empire they had built together. Horace's health then declined and he died eleven months later, joining the one from whom he had never been separated.

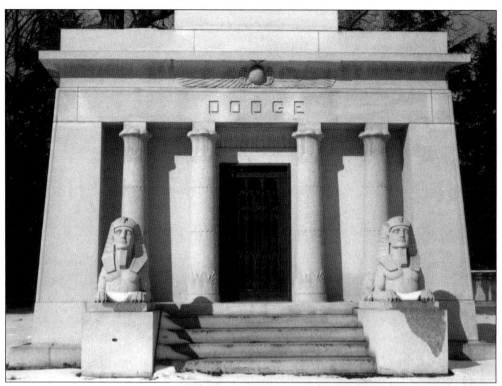

That bond between them is made more permanent within a monumental Egyptian Revival pyramid-like structure. Two matching sphinxes, which guard the entrance, could symbolize the strength and wisdom of the Dodge brothers. The doorway is framed with four papyrus-topped columns atop which the name has the same bold letters used in Dodge advertisements. The mausoleum was commissioned from the Lloyd brothers of Toledo, Ohio in 1913. As with Egyptian architecture, there is a sense of continuity in an after life with this impressive structure. (Photo courtesy Walter P. Reuther Library, Wayne State University.)

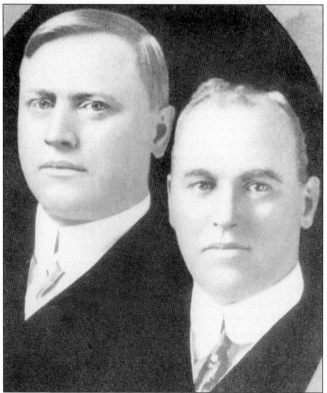

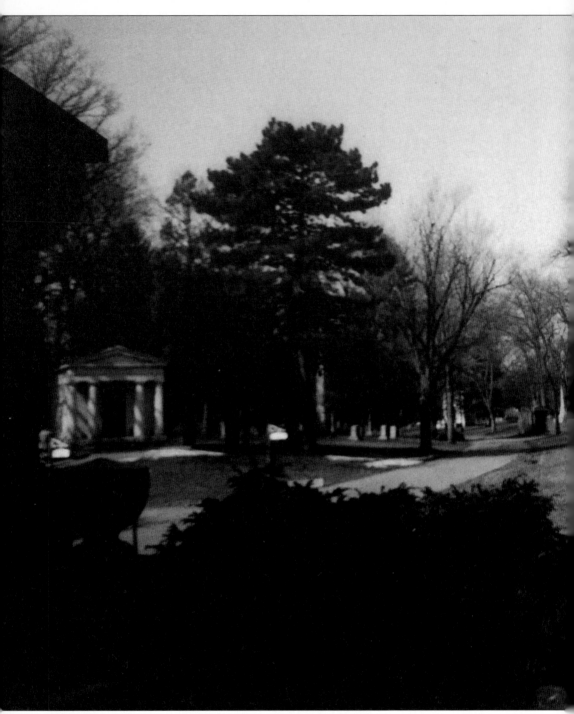

20C. Anna Thomson Dodge, 1871–1970. From humble beginnings in Detroit, Anna Thomson married Horace Dodge in 1896 and was his wife until his death in 1920. The Dodge Motor Company was sold to Chrysler in 1928 for a record $146 million, making Anna, and her sister-in-law, Matilda Dodge, very wealthy women. Anna proceeded to live a very lavish lifestyle building "Rose Terrace" in Grosse Pointe Farms, which was designed by Philadelphia

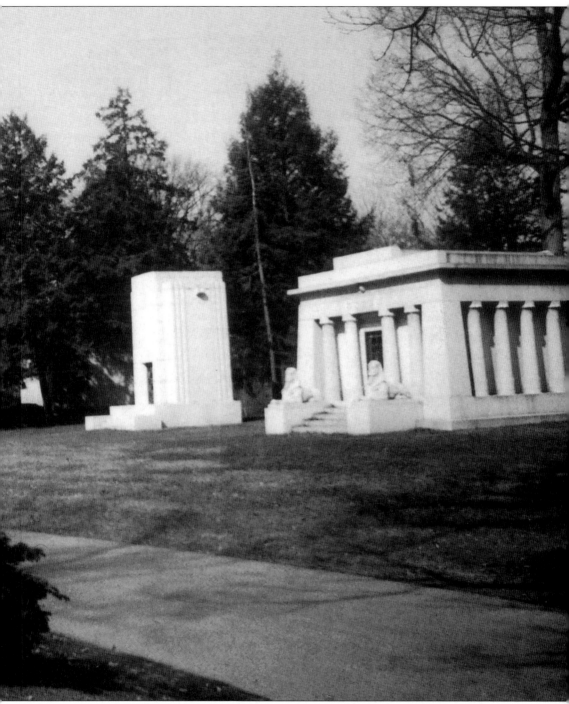

architect Horace Trumbauer in 1931. She spent an estimated $3 million furnishing the house with such luxuries as chairs with the monogram of Marie Antoinette and a bureau designed for Catherine the Great of Russia. The house was demolished in 1976 which was a loss to the architectural legacy of the Grosse Pointes.

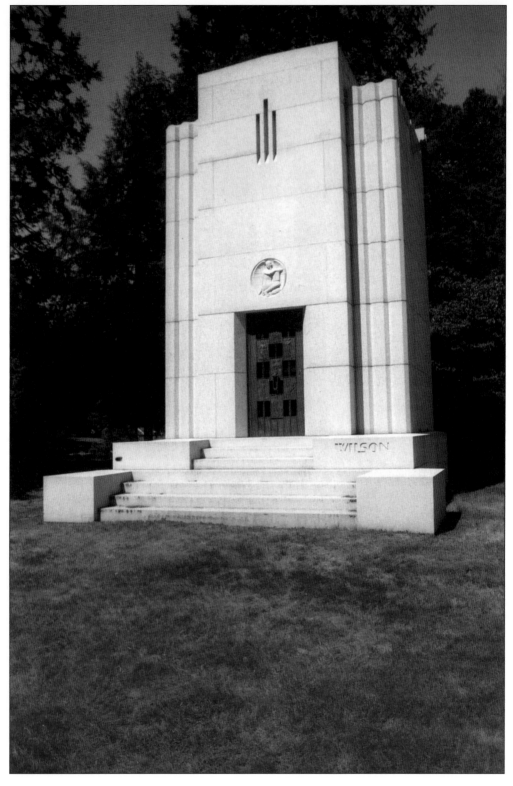

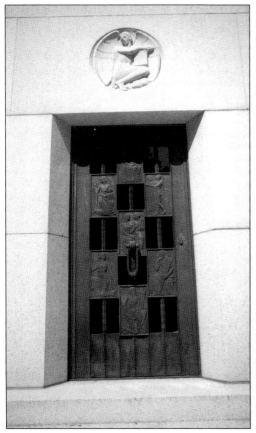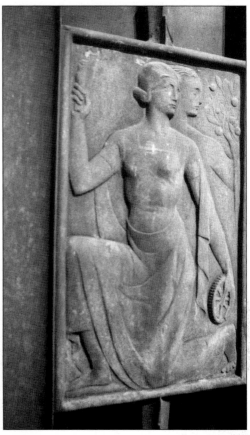

21. Matilda Dodge Wilson and Alfred Wilson, 1883–1967, 1880–1962. Matilda Rausch married John Dodge in 1907. After John's death in 1920, she went on to marry Alfred Wilson, a lumber merchant, in 1925. With her wealth, she had many charitable causes, most notably Oakland University in Rochester, which had been her 1500-acre estate until she bequeathed it for educational purposes.

The Wilson mausoleum is done in the Art Deco style with a vertical emphasis and sleek parallel straight lines in low relief. It was designed by New York architect William Henry Deacy and completed in 1939. The entrance doors, along with the sculptural medallion over the entrance, are the work of Detroit architectural sculptor Corrado Parducci, who also did the stonework on Mrs. Wilson's home, "Meadowbrook" in Rochester, Michigan. One of the panels shows Mrs. Wilson, with her second husband Alfred in profile behind her. Mrs. Wilson holds a wheel in her hand which symbolizes her early involvement with the automobile industry.

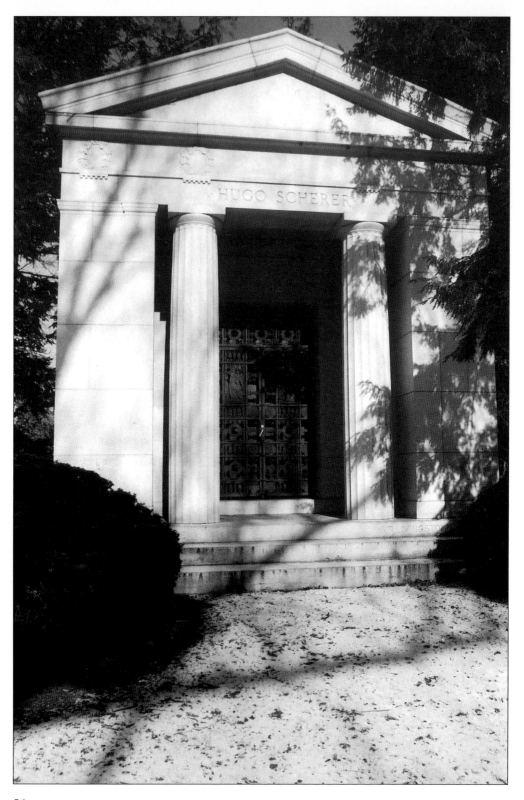

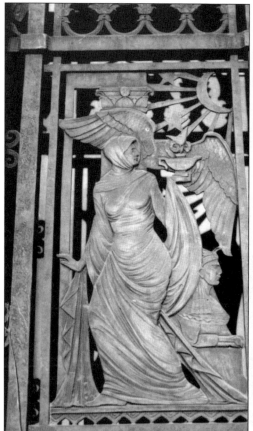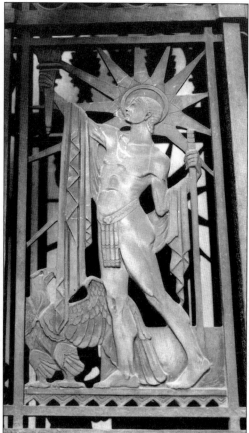

22. HUGO SCHERER, 1859–1923. Scherer started out in Detroit as a manufacturer and wholesaler of carriage trimmings in 1895. When the automobile came into general use, he met the demand for similar equipment. He went on to become President of the Detroit Forging Company, as well as the Michigan Steel Boat Company. Scherer owned several downtown Detroit buildings.

The Scherer mausoleum is designed in the Greek Revival style with Doric columns flanking the entry. It was designed by Detroit architect George Mason in 1925. On the base are two sculptured panels that portray classical meditative male figures. They were executed by Detroit architectural sculptor Corrado Parducci who referred to the figures as his personal interpretation of the Greek. (Photo courtesy Einar Kvaran.)

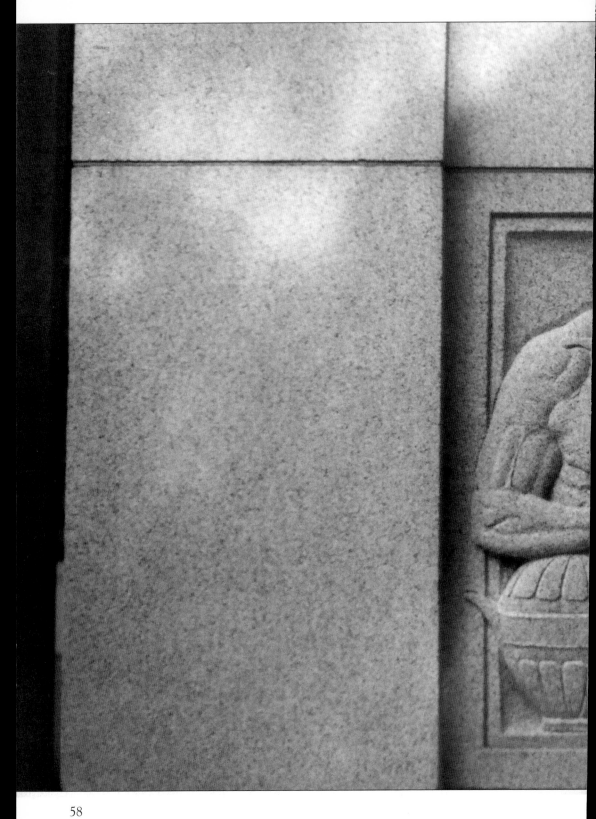

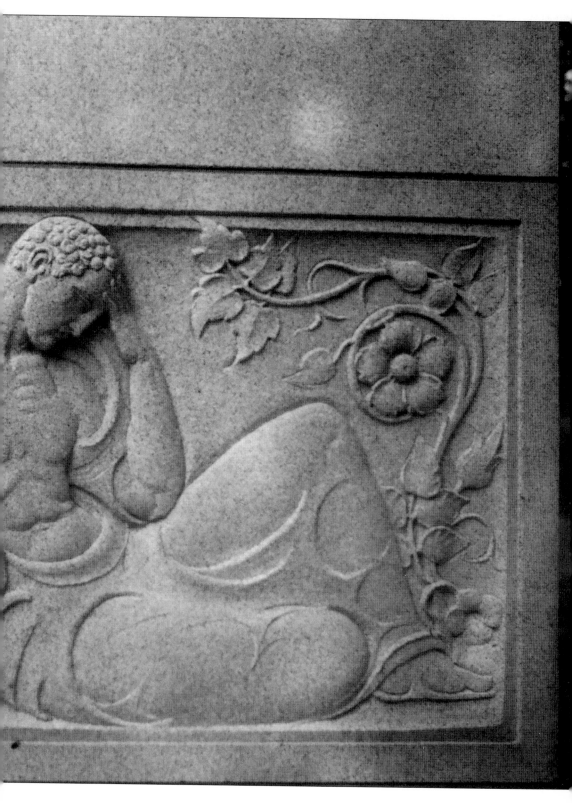

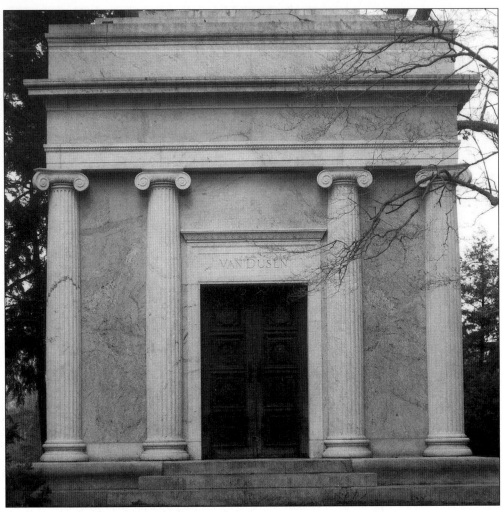

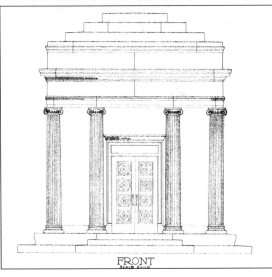

FRONT
SCALE ¾"=1'-0"

23. Charles Belden Van Dusen, 1871-1958. After coming to the S.S. Kresge Company in 1904, Van Dusen worked his way up through the ranks to succeed founder Sebastian Kresge as president (1925-1938). As a 33rd Degree Mason, he was involved in fund raising for the Masonic Temple in Detroit, the largest Masonic temple in the United States. A magnificent Neo-Gothic structure, the temple was designed by notable Detroit architect George D. Mason (mentor of Albert Kahn) in 1913. It was built at a cost of $2.5 million.

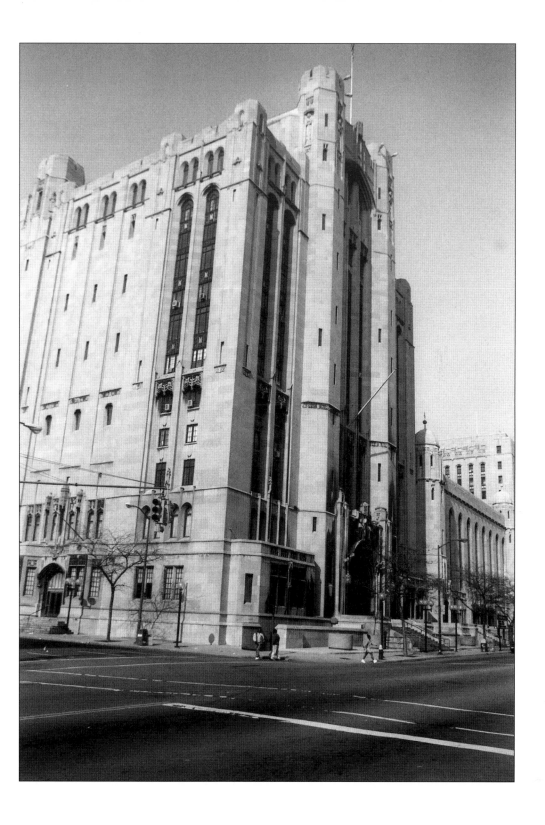

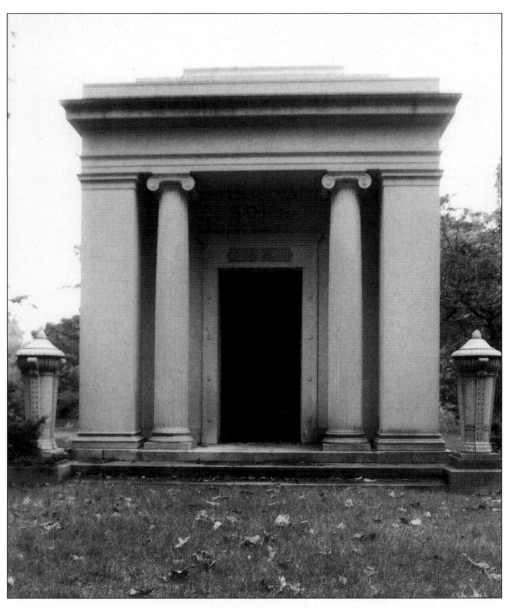

24. CHARLES B. BOHN, 1880–1953. Starting out at the age of 17, Bohn worked as a bookkeeper for a small Cleveland brass works where he picked up practical knowledge of the business. At the age of 20, with three companions, Bohn bought the company. Their foundry became the first to offer commercial aluminum castings. In 1918, Bohn organized the Charles B. Bohn Foundry in Detroit and, during World War I, furnished aluminum castings for the famous "Liberty" airplane engines. Five years later a merger served to form Bohn Aluminum and Brass. Bohn was the first independent foundry to commercialize aluminum castings which proved to be more vital to aviation than to the automobile industry. He pioneered in a number of aircraft developments, particularly those related to light metal engine parts.

The Bohn mausoleum is Classical Revival with Ionic columns flanking the doorway which has a bronze female figure in relief on the door, executed by Ben Johnson who worked for the Gorham Bronze Company. Inverted capped pedestals mark the entry.

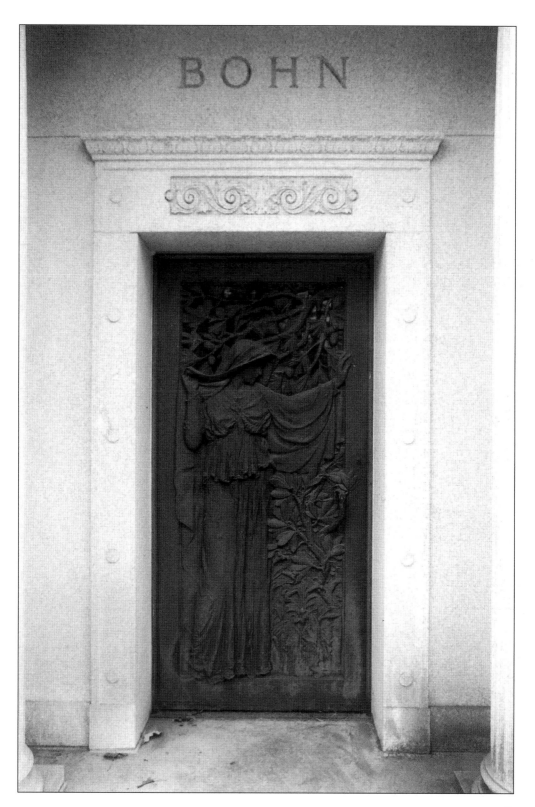

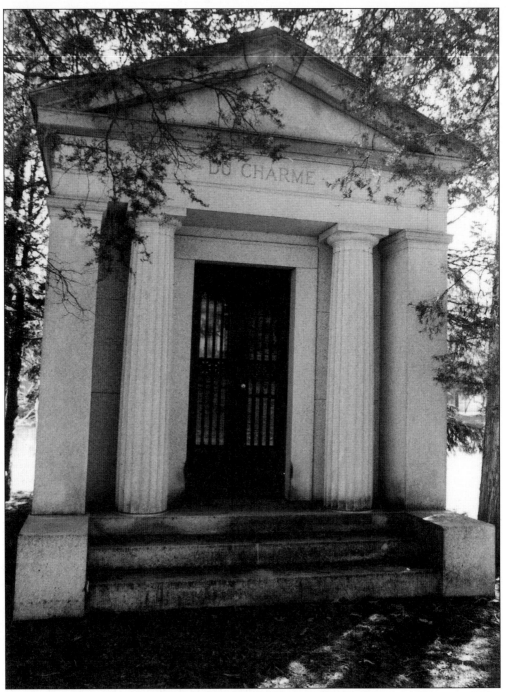

25. CHARLES ALBERT DUCHARME, 1858–1925. Charles Albert was a pivotal figure with the Michigan Stove Company, having risen from clerk to president over the course of 42 years. He followed in the footsteps of his father, Charles, who was one of the originators of the company, becoming president in 1871.

The Ducharme mausoleum is Greek Revival with the entrance flanked by Doric columns and square piers on the corners.

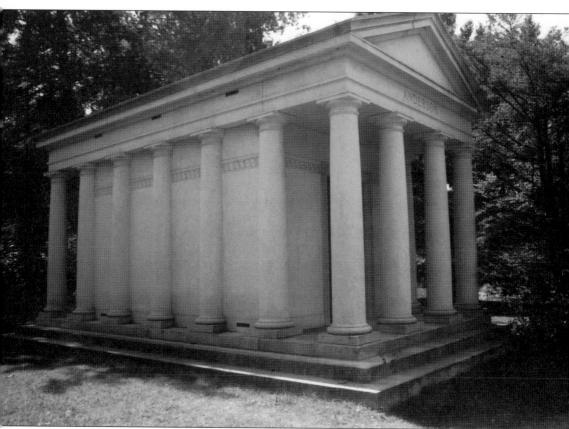

26. JOHN WENDELL ANDERSON, 1867–1946. Anderson was a successful Detroit lawyer. He was one of the original charter shareholders of the Ford Motor Company and served as attorney for the company. In 1903, he invested $5,000 in 50 shares of Ford stock. The money was loaned to Anderson by his father, who had borrowed it himself. John Wendell sold his stock to Ford in 1919 for $12.5 million.

The Anderson mausoleum is Classical Revival in the Roman style. It is the work of the Lloyd Brothers Monument Company. There is a portico on the front with columns on the side that are attached to the wall. This motif suggests that the designer used a Roman temple as a prototype, undoubtedly, the Maison Carree in Nimes, France, 16 B.C., one of the most famous of antique temples. However, whereas the Romans preferred to use the more elaborate Corthinian order, this structure has the simpler Doric.

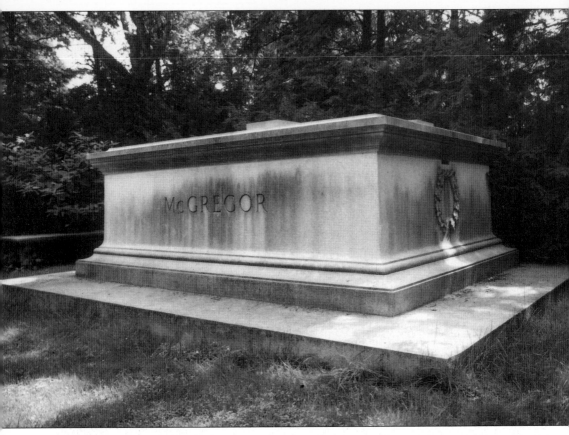

27. TRACY AND KATHERINE MCGREGOR, 1869–1936, 1873-1954. Tracy Mc Gregor can be described as a humane philanthropist. Following his father's death in 1891, Tracy left college and came to Detroit to take over the operation of a mission, the McGregor Institute (1890–1936) for homeless men founded by his father. An estimated 700,000 men were housed and fed by the Institute.

He and his wife, Katherine, then went on to improve the betterment of humankind. They established the McGregor Fund in 1925 which supported the indigent, provided relief of the sick, and sustained higher education. Their aim was "To relieve misfortunes and promote the well-being of humanity." The fund continues today as a major philanthropic organization in such areas as human services, education, health care, arts and culture, and public benefits.

The McGregor sarcophagus is simple yet has a monumentality that expresses the magnitude of their giving nature.

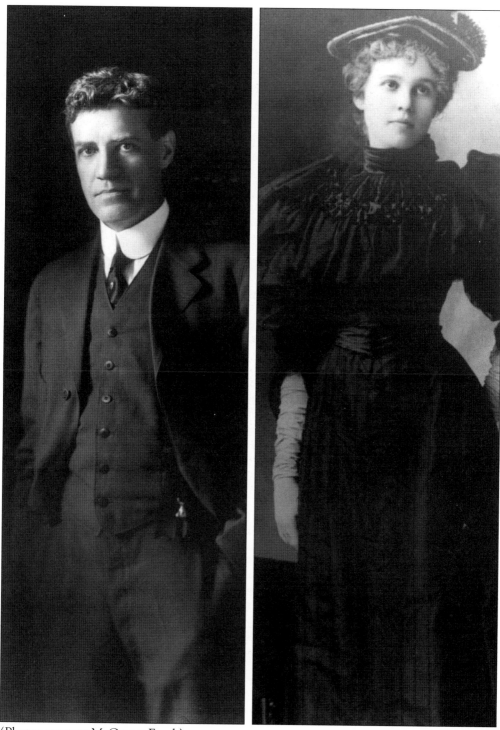

(Photos courtesy McGregor Fund.)

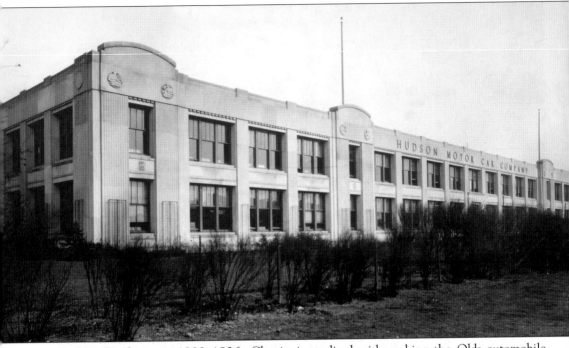

28. ROY D. CHAPIN, 1880–1936. Chapin is credited with making the Olds automobile famous when he drove it from Detroit to New York in 1901 for the Second Annual Auto show. Auto makers drew attention to their auto with promotional road trips. It was the longest automobile trip at that time. Chapin ran into muddy, rutted roads. He then took the relatively smooth tow path of the Erie Canal, although battling mule drivers along the way. He arrived at the Waldorf-Astoria Hotel, in New York City, after an arduous nine-day, 14-mile-per-hour journey with a one-cylinder engine. He was to meet Ransom E. Olds at the hotel. Since he was dirty and greasy from the trip, the doorman asked him to use the service entrance. Thereafter, Chapin had garnered scads of publicity for the curved dash car.

Chapin was General Sales Manager of the Olds Motor Works in 1904. In 1908, he became Treasurer and General Manager of the E.R. Thomas Motor Car Company. He then went on, in 1909, to form the Hudson Motor Car Company (1909–1957) which was named for its primary financial backer, Detroit retail store merchant Joseph L. Hudson. In spite of the fact that the automobile industry was still highly speculative, the company got off to a rousing start. Its first year in business posted 4,000 sales. Chapin was president of the Hudson Motor Car Company (1910–36). In 1910, the company moved into its new Albert Kahn-designed plant on East Jefferson. Factories, along with automobiles, became a new design frontier in the United States. The simple design of the Hudson factory was expressive of the concrete frame construction.

The design of the original car and manufacture had been drawn up by Chapin and Howard E. Coffin, who had received their training and inspiration from the Olds enterprise. First the company produced a low-priced roadster model, and then went on to become the largest manufacturer of moderately-priced cars. The company got off to a very good start. In 1909, the business posted sales of 4,000. By 1929, Hudson rated third in sales behind Ford and Chevrolet. Awakened by the frustrating experience of driving to the New York auto show, Chapin spent the rest of his life campaigning for better roads. In 1913, he became a member of the Lincoln Highway Association, which promoted the first intercontinental highway from New York to San Francisco. It was the Hudson car that held the transcontinental record on the Lincoln Highway. (Photo courtesy Walter P. Reuther Library, Wayne State University.)

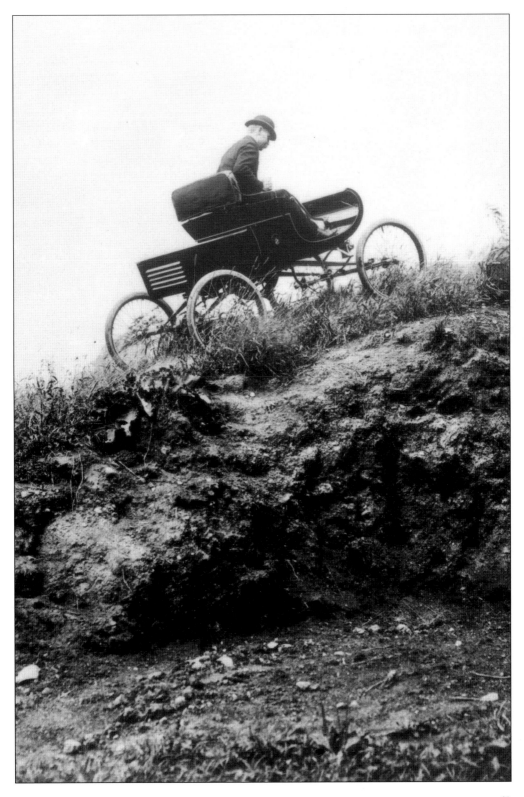

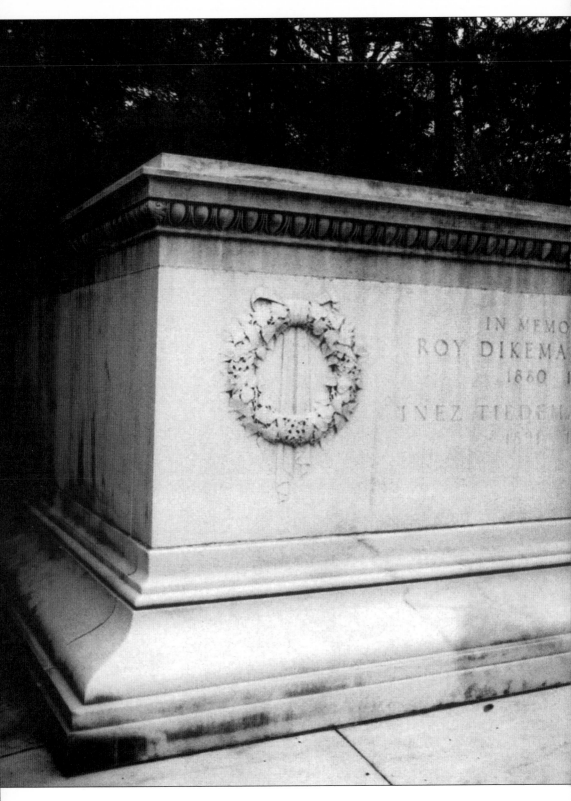

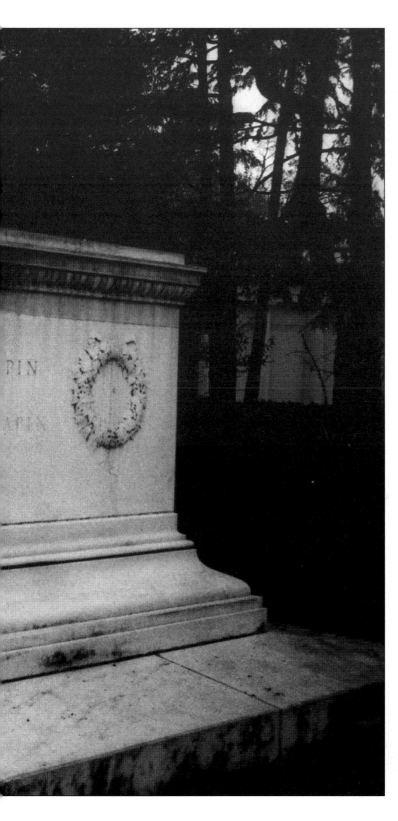

Chapin is interred in this marble sarcophagus, along with his wife, Inez. The classic molding furnishes the decoration on a restful and dignified design of the structure. Wreaths on either side of the names symbolize victory in death.

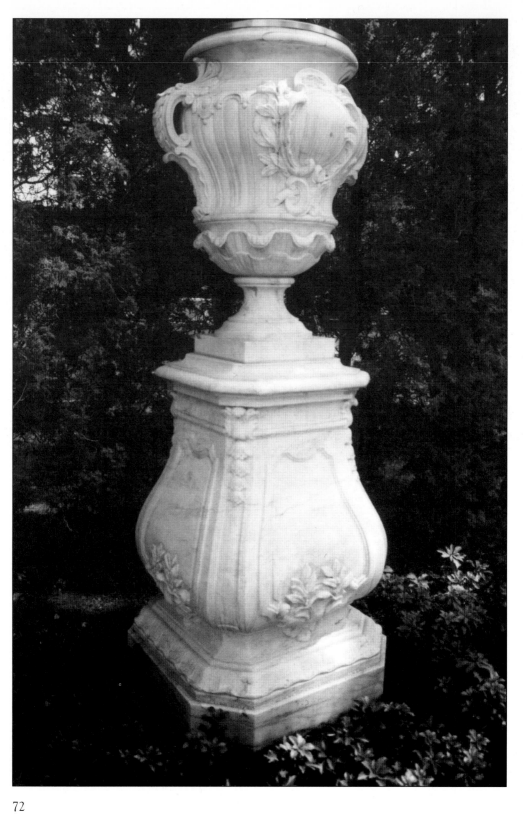

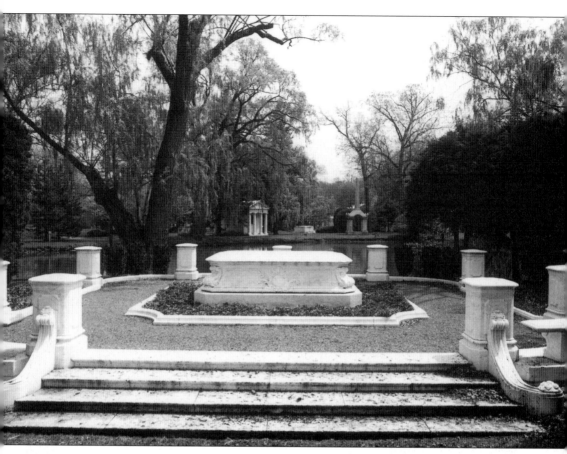

29. ERNEST AND JOSEPHINE KANZLER, 1892–1967, 1891–1954. Ernest Kanzler was production manager at the Ford Motor Company (1920–26), establishing the first Production Control Department for the company. He became Vice President and Director of the Lincoln Motor Car Company (1923–26). Then he was fired by Henry Ford because he dared to tell Henry the Model T had to be replaced with something more up-to-date. He went on to organize the Guardian Detroit Bank with Edsel Ford in 1928. It was the nucleus of the Guardian Detroit Union Group, a holding company encompassing 25 Michigan banks.

His wife, Josephine, was the sister of Eleanor Clay Ford. The Kanzlers were patrons of art at the Detroit Institute of Arts where Josephine was instrumental in promoting modern art.

Measuring approximately 50 feet by 50 feet, the Kanzler plot is reminiscent of an 18th century French formal garden. It was fabricated by the Lloyd brothers of Toledo, Ohio. The inspiration for the site was a rare antique urn from the Louis XV period, which Mr. Kanzler bought when he was in Paris. The base for the original urn, and its companion urn and base on the other side, were cut in France of matching marble. The sarcophagus is carved from one piece of marble. The Vermont Marble Company supplied the marble and stated that it is one of the most elaborately designed memorials to pass through their plant. New York architect William Henry Deacy served as a design consultant. The Kanzlers now lie at rest in the same grand style that they lived.

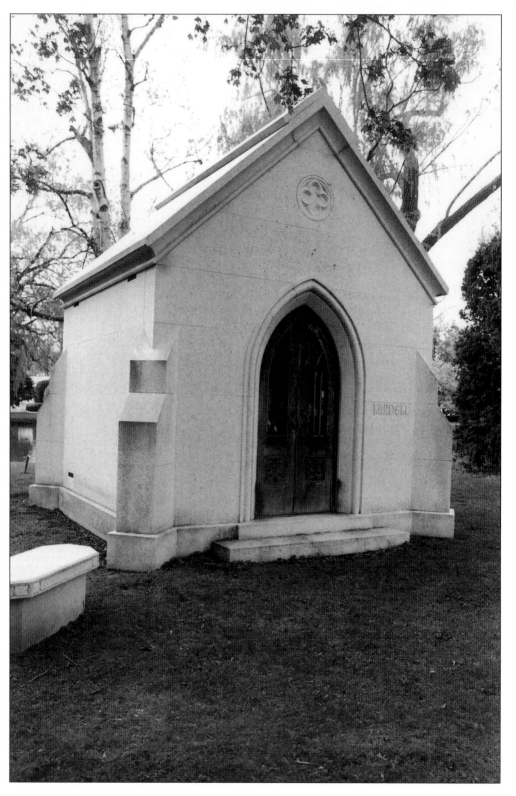

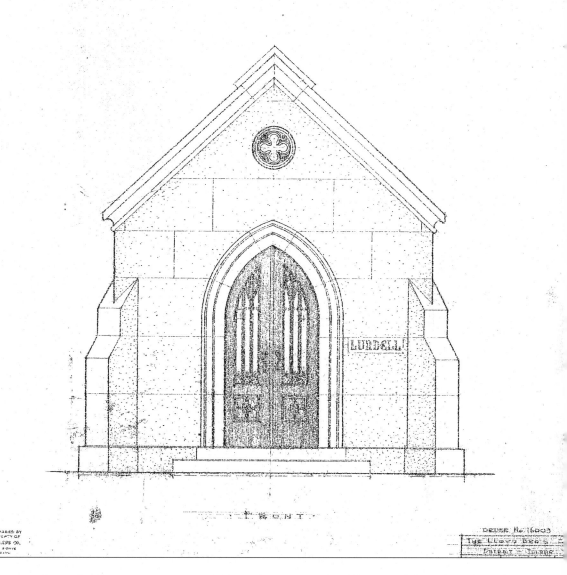

Reproduced with signage reading: **LUNDELL**

FRONT

30. OTTO AMANDUS LUNDELL, 1878–1940. A native of Sweden, Lundell graduated with a degree in mechanical engineering from the University of Gottenberg. He migrated to the United States where he took a job as a shop manager with the Michigan Tool Company in Detroit.

The mausoleum, fabricated by the Lloyd brothers, is Gothic Revival with a pointed arch marking the entry, above which is a Gothic quatrefoil in relief.

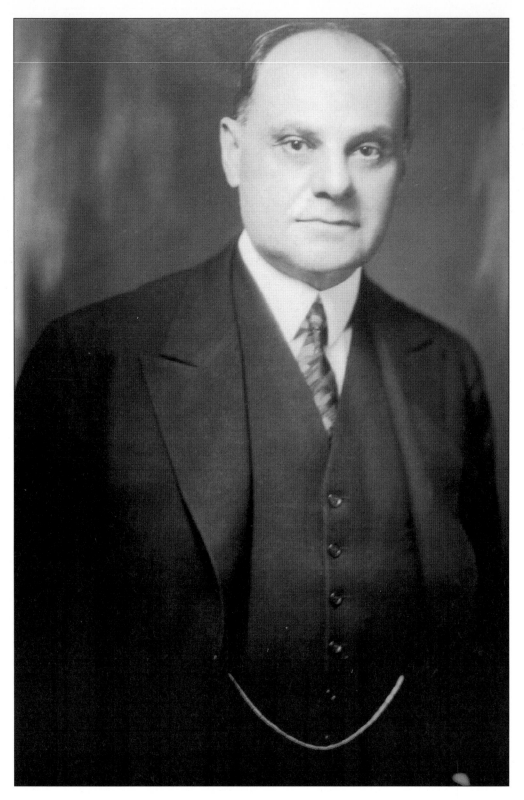

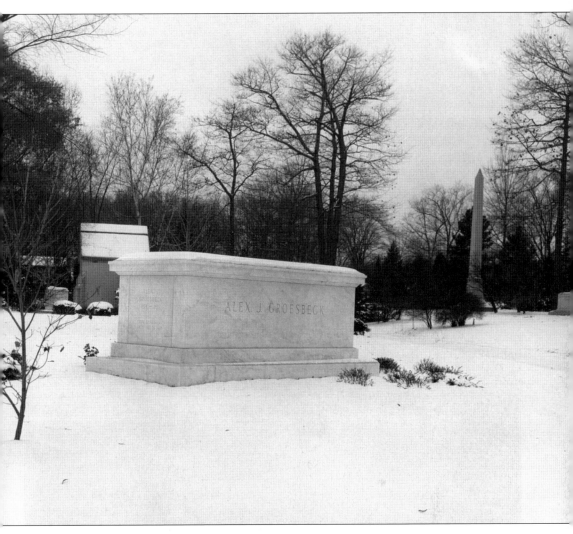

31. ALEX J. GROESBECK, 1873–1953. Groesbeck had a distinguished law career in Detroit. After serving as state Attorney General (1917–20), he became the 30th Governor of Michigan (1921–1926) for three successive terms. In 1922, Groesbeck appointed James Couzens to replace Truman Newberry, who resigned as U.S. Senator. He saw in Couzens the managerial skills that Couzens used at Ford Motor Company and also imparted as Detroit Police Commissioner and Mayor. The Groesbeck administration was noted for governmental reorganization, prison reform, and bringing Michigan "out of the mud" by initiating the state's modern system of highways. In 1927, he returned to Detroit where he retained an active interest in public affairs.

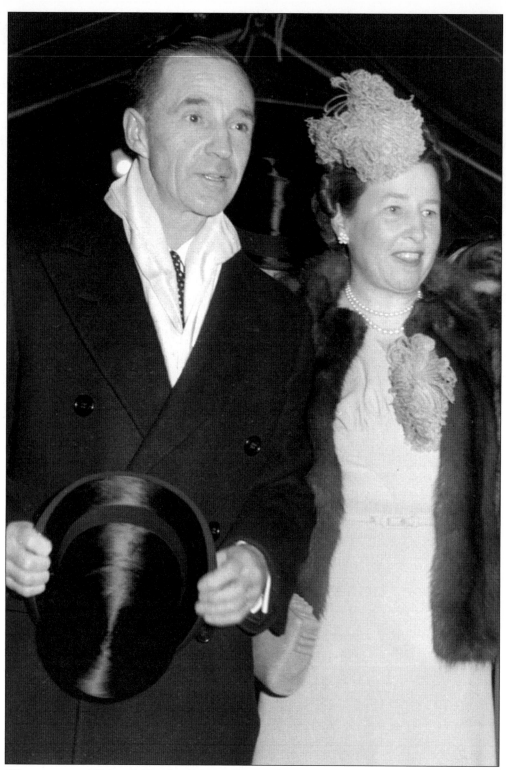

(Photo courtesy Walter P. Reuther Library, Wayne State University.)

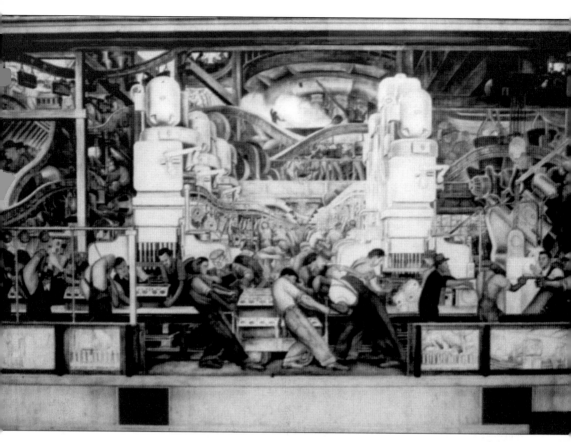

32. EDSEL BRYANT AND ELEANOR CLAY FORD, 1893–1943, 1896–1976. The development of Edsel Ford coincided with the development of the automobile. During his lifetime, there was never a time that he wasn't involved with the automotive world. He was the president of the Ford Motor Company from 1919 to 1943. One of Edsel's more important contributions to the company was an eye for design, which he influenced and encouraged. He was instrumental in the birth of the Lincoln Zephyr (1935), which the Museum of Modern Art called the first streamlined car. It was the hit of the 1936 New York Auto Show. In 1939, Edsel instructed Ford's head designer, Bob Gregorie, to build a one-of-a-kind "strictly continental" car, which resulted in the Lincoln Continental.

In addition to his creative involvement with Ford, Edsel served as President of the Detroit Arts Commission in 1931, during which time he underwrote the cost of hiring Mexican artist Diego Rivera to paint the famous industrial murals at the Detroit Institute of Arts. Those murals might well be the memorial that the quiet, self-effacing son of Henry Ford considered most fitting for Detroit. During the same time period, the Great Depression, he and his wife Eleanor paid staff salaries to keep the museum open for the public.

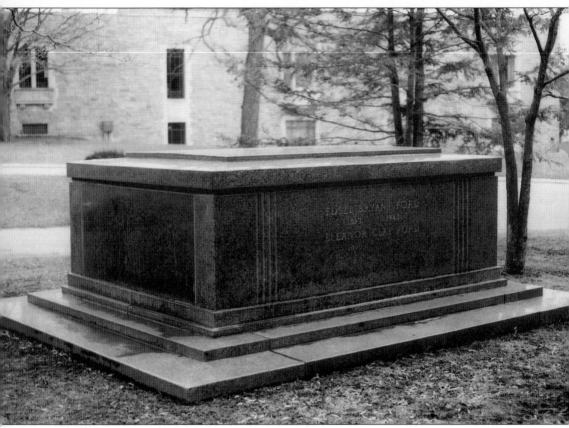

After Edsel's death, Eleanor Ford continued as a major benefactor of the Detroit Institute of Arts. She established the Eleanor Clay Ford Fund for African Art, making it one of the country's leading collections. Mr. and Mrs. Ford were among Detroit's earliest collectors of African art. Mrs. Ford was also instrumental in the founding of the Archives of American Art, now a part of the Smithsonian in Washington, D.C.

There is an elegant simplicity and dignity about the polished black granite Ford sarcophagus that suggests the unassuming nature of the Fords, as opposed to the other more ornate monuments and mausoleums.

Three
Section C
(Main Mausoleum)
Sections 40, 24, 38, and 41

(Plots 34–41)

34. Alfred Lucking, 1856–1929. Lucking was a Detroit attorney who, for 10 years, was chief counsel for the Ford Motor Company and personal attorney to Henry Ford. During that time he handled the $1 million libel suit of Ford against the *Chicago Tribune*. Ford won in principal. The jury found the newspaper guilty and fined it 6¢. Lucking had also represented the Ford Motor Company in 1916 against an injunction sought by John and Horace Dodge to compel the company to pay dividends. This ultimately led to Ford buying out the stockholders.

Lucking was chairman of many Democratic conventions and served as a member of Congress for the First Michigan District (1903–05).

The monument is an obelisk with a concave base which is a modern detail. The top of the pedestal is decorated on the four lateral edges with a lotus buds in relief.

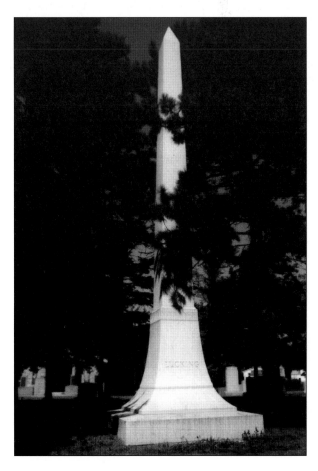

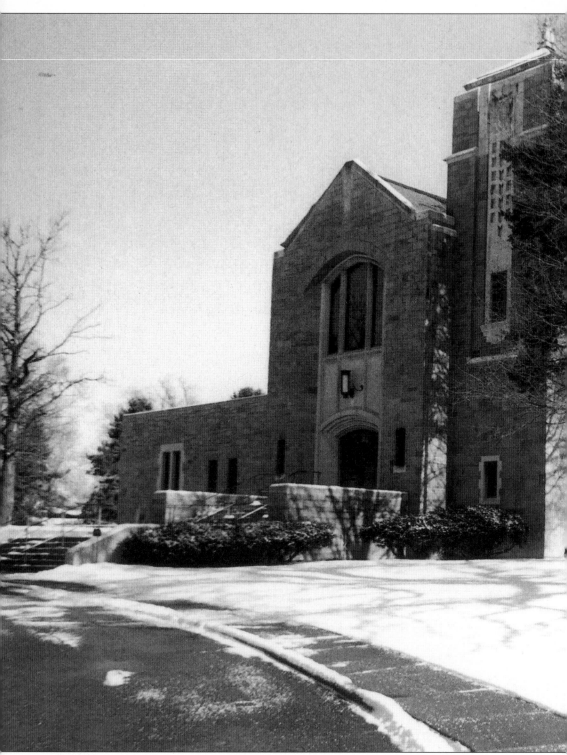

33. Community Mausoleum, Harley, Ellington, Day, Architects, 1941. This is a

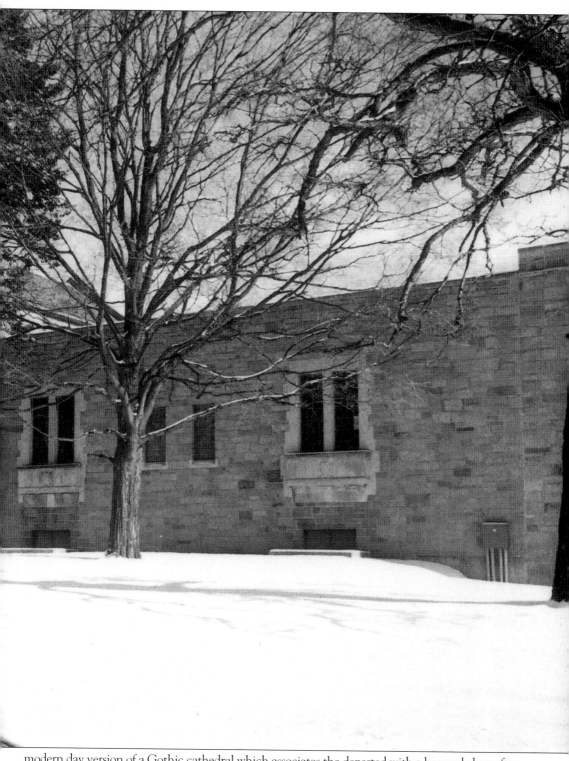

modern day version of a Gothic cathedral which associates the departed with a heavenly hereafter.

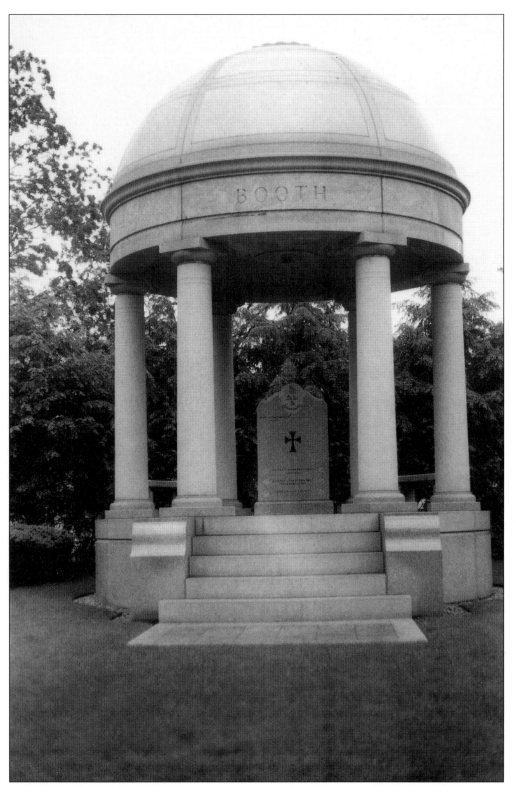

35. JOHN LORD BOOTH, 1907-1994.
Booth was President of Booth
Broadcasting, which owned several radio
stations in Michigan. He was also a
pioneer in cable television.

The Booth plot is marked with a
cylindrical temple-like peristyle structure
capped by a masonry dome. Inside, a
marker defines Booth as a man of energy
and invincible determination. Above is
the family crest of three boars' heads with
the family motto "Quod ero spero," which
translates from the Latin to "what I shall
be I hope."

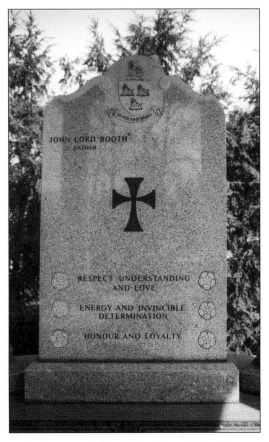

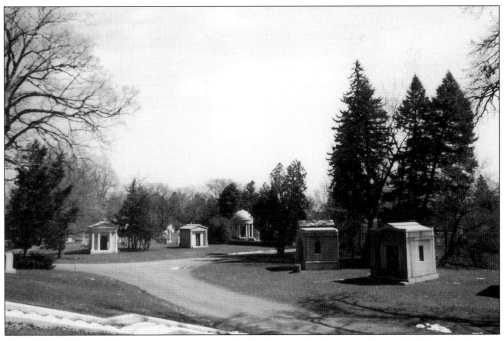

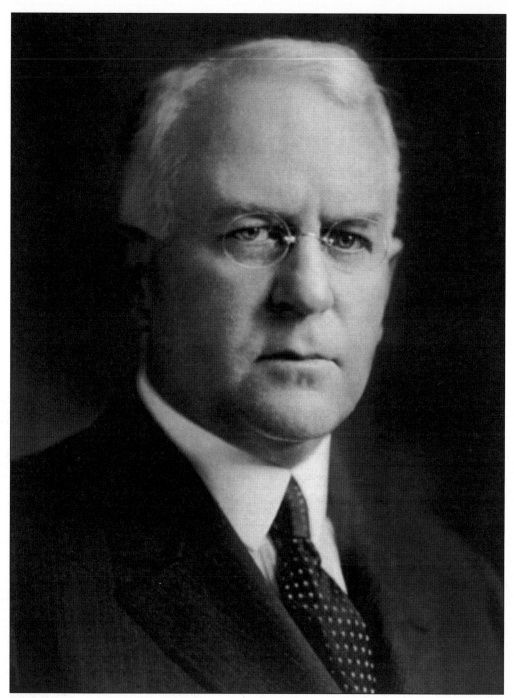

36. JAMES COUZENS, 1872–1936. James Couzens was born in Chatham, Ontario, Canada. He recalled the time when his family didn't have enough money to own a kerosene lamp. Perhaps being impoverished led Couzens to become a man of higher aspirations. He has been noted for his competence, aggressiveness, and working sagacity. He recalled later, "All my life, from the day I was born, has been a struggle. Only in the fight to get things did I ever find any satisfaction—and once I got them, there was no thrill."

Couzens entered into a partnership with Henry Ford in 1903 as Treasurer of the Ford Motor Company. He is considered the man responsible for the success of the company in its early years, establishing a network of agents to sell Henry Ford's cars. He is also claimed to be responsible for the $5-a-day wage plan which stirred the world in 1914. He became a principle stockholder in the Ford Motor Company and went on to serve as vice president and general manager. Noted for his managerial skills, he was second in command through many of the Model T years.

Couzens quit Ford in 1915. In 1919, he sold his stock in the company for $30 million, since Ford wanted to gain 100 percent ownership of the company. Couzens was one of the last stockholders to hold out. He returned a large portion of what he received to the community as a philanthropist. As well, he went into public life serving as Police Commissioner of Detroit (1916–18) and Mayor of the City of Detroit (1918–22). As Mayor of Detroit, he fought successfully for the municipal ownership of the streetcar system. He then went on to serve as a U.S. Senator (1922–36).

Upon his death in 1936, President Franklin Roosevelt paid tribute to Couzens as "... a leader whose convictions were part of the best America aspires and his courage matched his idealism." The Couzens mausoleum is, indeed, a monument that reflects his achievements. Built of granite, it is an outstanding example of the Greek Revival style with symmetrically spaced, fluted columns capped by Doric capitols that completely surround the structure. It is considered one of the largest mausoleums in the Detroit area and could be looked upon as a mini-version of the Parthenon from the Golden Age of Greece. The mausoleum was designed in 1920, and the steps in 1926, by Detroit architect Albert Kahn, who also designed the Couzens house in Detroit in 1910. It only seems logical that Kahn would also design Couzens' place of repose.

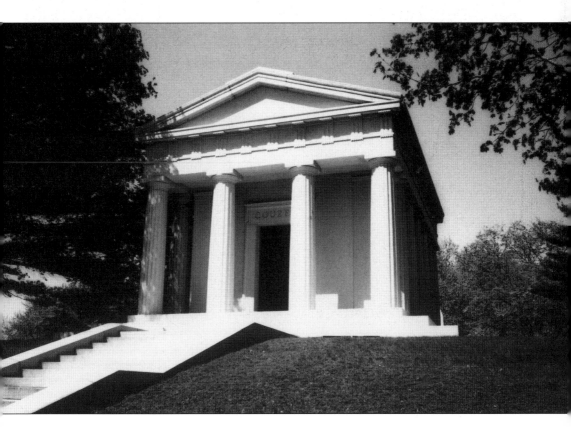

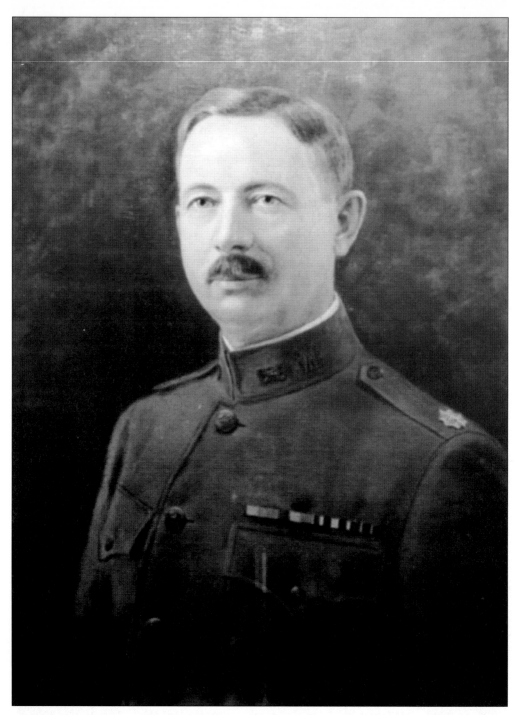

37. EDWARD EDGAR HARTWICK, 1871–1918. A graduate of the West Point Military Academy in 1893, Hartwick fought in the Spanish-American War. He organized the Hartwick Lumber Company in Detroit in 1909. Then he volunteered for active service at the outbreak of World War I, in which he oversaw the laying of miles of railroad track and sidings for U.S. Army troops. He died of natural causes while on active duty. Hartwick State Pine Park, which

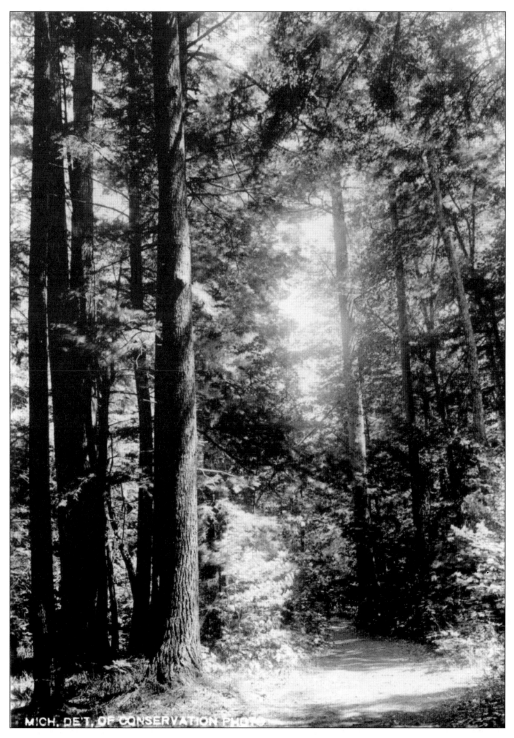

MICH. DEPT. OF CONSERVATION PHOTO

bears his name, is the largest state park in the lower peninsula of Michigan. The acreage of stately white pines was donated to the state in 1927 by Karen Hartwick, in memory of her husband. (Photos courtesy of State Archives of Michigan.)

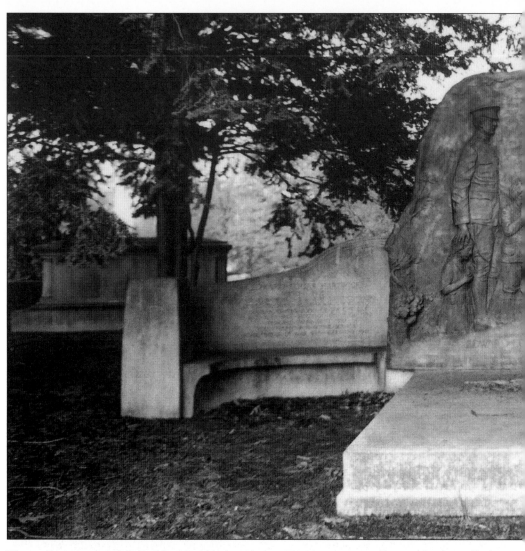

The monument was designed by New York architect W. Liance Cottrell in 1920. Cottrell also designed the Pennsylvania Monument at Gettysburg National Military Park in 1910. The bronze relief sculpture was executed by New York sculptor Julius Loester who also did the Civil War Monument at Vicksburg, Mississippi, which commemorates the Wisconsin militia who died there. The Hartwick monument shows a full-length soldier, perhaps Hartwick, standing in a protective capacity over two orphaned children who have lost their father in the war. A beautiful poem, "Our Dead Overseas" by American poet Edwin Markham, appears beside the figures and serves as a tribute to Hartwick.

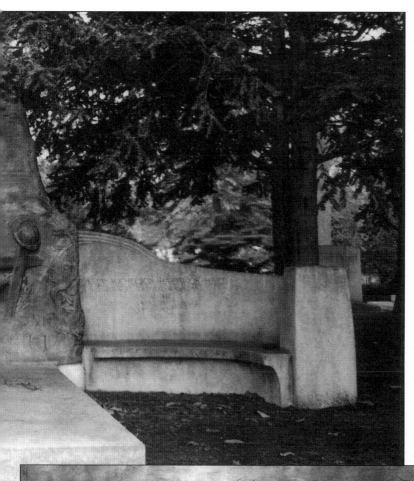

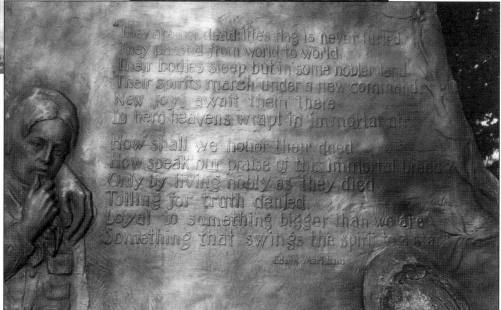

They are not dead: life's flag is never furled
They passed from world to world.
Their bodies sleep but in some nobler land
Their spirits march under a new command.
New joys await them there
In hero heavens wrapt in immortal air

How shall we honor their deed
How speak our praise of this immortal breed
Only by living nobly as they died
Toiling for truth denied,
Loyal to something bigger than we are
Something that swings the spirit to a star

Edwin Markham

91

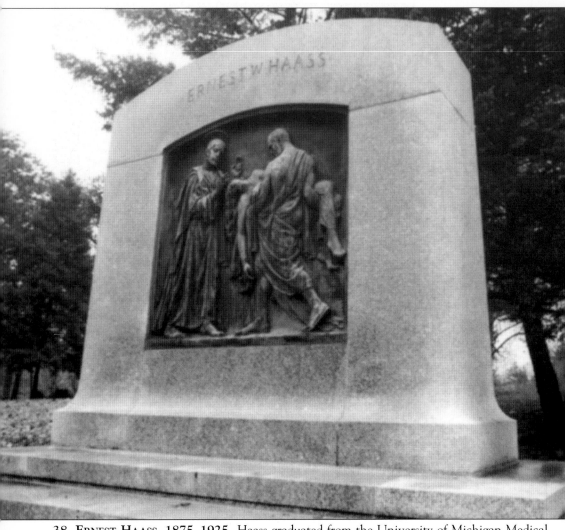

38. Ernest Haass, 1875–1925. Haass graduated from the University of Michigan Medical School in 1892. He practiced medicine in Detroit where he was an attending physician at Harper Hospital. He was considered one of the best-informed medical men in the country. His dedication as a doctor is commemorated with this sculptural relief on the tombstone that portrays Christ healing the sick. It was executed by notable American sculptor Charles Keck, who is best known for his statue of Booker T. Washington at the Tuskegee Institute in Alabama.

As inscribed on the back of the monument, Haass wanted to be remembered as "devoting his life to the good of mankind," which he did, of course, as a dedicated medical doctor.

39. GEORGE RUPERT FINK, 1886–1962. Fink was born outside Pittsburgh in the heart of the steel region. He began his career as a youthful "door puller" on the open hearths at West Penn Steel, whereupon the production of steel must have been instilled. Then he went on to become a salesman with the Allegheny Steel Corporation. He moved to Detroit where he became a major figure in steel production. He formed the Michigan Steel Company, devoted primarily to rolling auto body sheets. His real ambition was to create a firm that

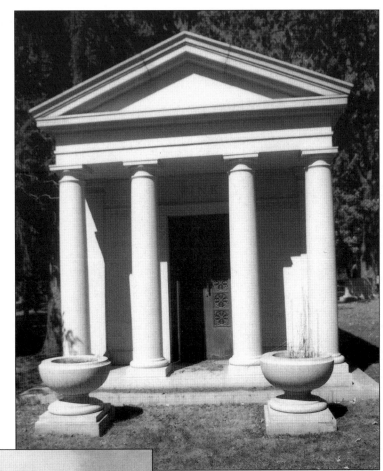

could make its own steel; consequently, Great Lakes Steel was born with Fink as president. Great Lakes Steel then became a subsidiary of the National Steel Corporation, Michigan's largest producer of steel, of which Fink became president.

The Fink mausoleum is Egyptian Revival with a scarab prominently displayed over the front entrance. The scarab symbolized the renewal of life to the Egyptians, since it rolled a ball of dung in which another scarab was born. (Photo courtesy Walter P. Reuther Library, Wayne State University.)

93

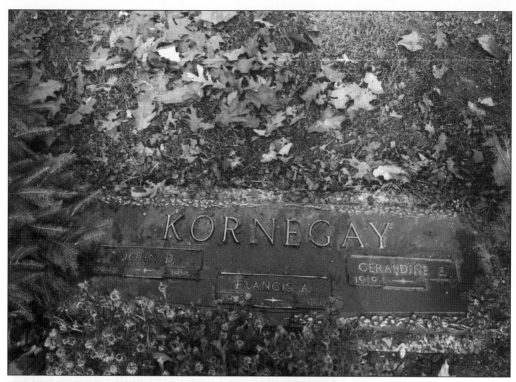

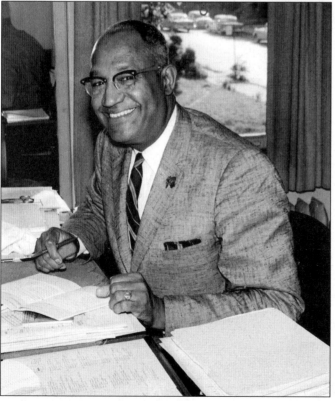

40. Francis Kornegay, 1913–2000. Kornegay began work with the Detroit Urban League in 1944 and went on to become its director (1960–78). He teamed up with the city and big business to improve the quality of life for the African-American community in the city. He had the ear of Henry Ford II. As well, he is credited with helping the first African-Americans secure jobs at Detroit Edison and the Bank of the Commonwealth. He served as President of the Michigan HMO Plans, what is now known as the Omnicare plan. (Photo courtesy Walter P. Reuther Library, Wayne State University.)

Four

SECTIONS 24, 25, 26, AND 23

(PLOTS 42–49)

41. PERCY W. GROSE, 1881–1934. Grose was a delegate to the Democratic National Convention in 1916 when President Woodrow Wilson was re-nominated and the Women's Suffrage Movement was endorsed.

This is a classically conceived monument with Doric columns flanking the four corners. The laurel wreath dates back to ancient Greek times and was adopted into the Christian religion as a symbol of salvation and protection.

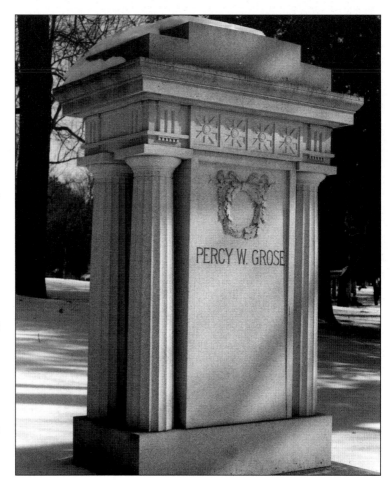

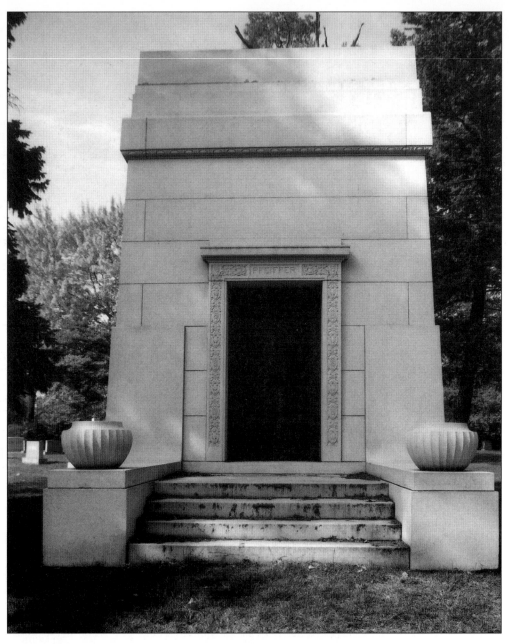

43. CONRAD PFEIFFER, 1854–1911. Pfeiffer was an emigrant from the German province of Hessen where he was born. When he came to America in 1871, at the age of 17, his education was limited. Germans comprised 15 percent of Detroit, with an American-German bank, a German newspaper, and many breweries owned by Germans. Pfeiffer entered into the career of brewing at the age of 27 in 1881, when he learned the brewing trade from the Kling Brewery in Detroit. In 1889, he founded his own company, the C. Pfeiffer Brewing Company, which was incorporated as a stock company in 1902. Conrad had the help of his nephew, Martin Breitmeyer, whose family provided the necessary financial backing. Breitmeyer assumed the position of bookkeeper of the company, then went on to become treasurer and vice-president.

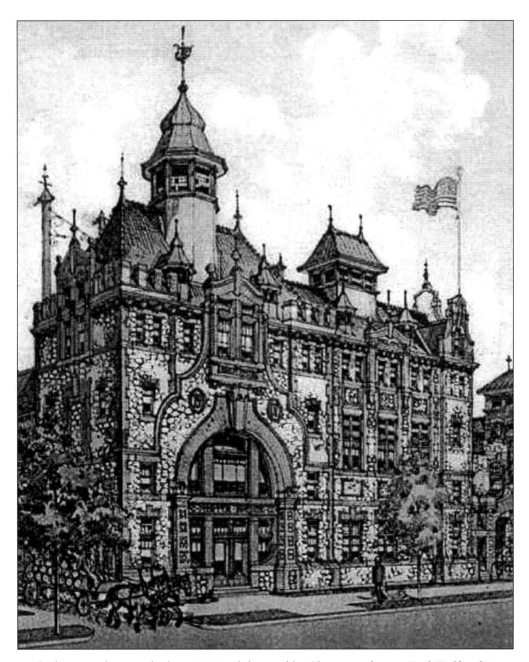

The brewery plant was built in 1899 and designed by Chicago architects Fred Wolf and Louis Lehle, who specialized in breweries. The building was in the Romanesque Revival and Bavarian castle styles with polychromatic and muscular details (now demolished). Wolf was German-born, as were many of his clients. He studied at a technical school in Karlsruhe, Germany, and apprenticed as an architect and mechanical engineer. Lehle was born in Ulm, Germany, and studied at the University of Stuttgart.

The Pfeiffer mausoleum is an impressive limestone structure with canted walls that almost suggest a pyramid-like shape. Delicate floral detail in relief defines the doorway with the surname overhead.

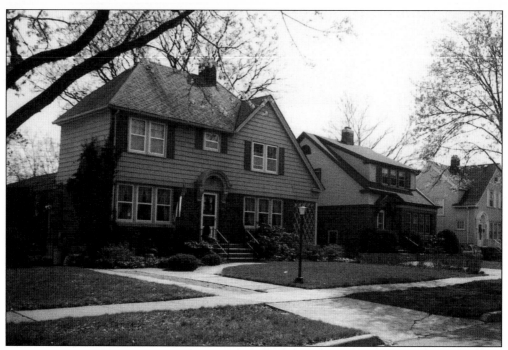

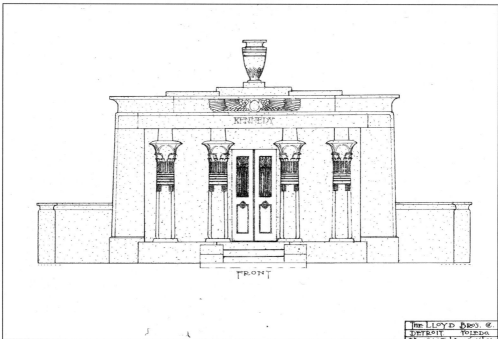

44. James and Charles Kennedy, 1864–1927, 1883–1948. The Kennedy brothers were both medical doctors. They gave up their practices to invest in the real estate market, developing and platting several subdivisions in the Dearborn area. One was the Dearborn Tractor subdivision for Ford employees who were renting houses in Detroit, which was a one-hour trip by streetcar to Dearborn. Ford felt housing should be closer to work, which he initiated. The price range of the houses was $7–8000.

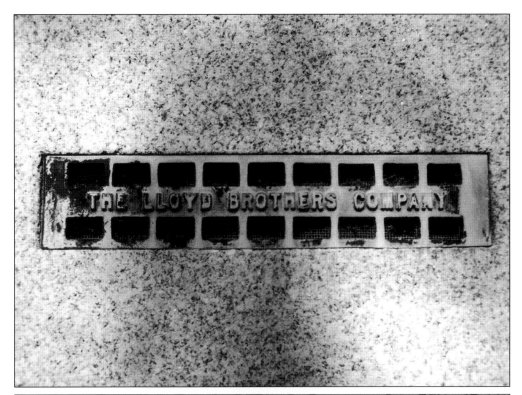

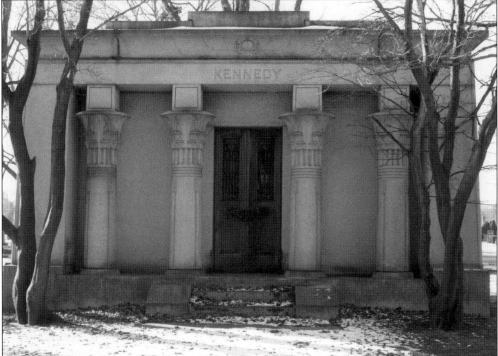

The Kennedy mausoleum is Egyptian Revival with four imposing columns capped by papyrus capitals. It was built by the Lloyd Brothers.

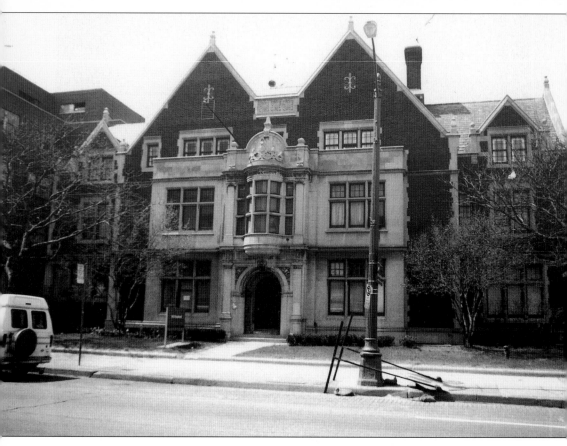

42. LEMUEL WARNER BOWEN, 1857–1925. In 1902, Bowen was one of the financial backers of the Henry Ford Company, as well when it was formerly the Detroit Automobile Company. Bowen, along with the other investors, had considered quitting the automobile industry since Ford was then more interested in racing cars. After a confrontation, Henry withdrew from the company, along with his name. The investors then called in automotive machinist Henry Leland who encouraged them to stay on and supplied them with an engine that provided more power. Faith was restored. The company went on to become Cadillac, at the suggestion of Leland, named after the French explorer Antoine de la Mothe Cadillac who founded Detroit in 1701. This was timely since Detroit had just celebrated its 200th anniversary. Thus, the first Cadillac was produced by Henry's one-time backers one year later in 1902. It was almost an exact duplicate of Ford's first car, excepting the engine. Bowen became president until the company was bought by General Motors in 1909.

Bowen was also General Manager of the D.M. Ferry seed company, becoming president in 1907. With his success in business, Bowen built a magnificent house at 1145, now 5435, Woodward Avenue, designed by Detroit architect George D. Mason in 1912. The fine stonework of the central panel stands out against the brickwork of the main body of the house with its steep roof and gables.

The Bowen monument was designed in 1927 by Philadelphia architect Paul Phillipe Cret, who also designed the Detroit Institute of Arts (1922). It is reminiscent of an Italian Renaissance sarcophagus—on the front are fluted pilasters, with claw feet on the bottom. The pilasters frame two angelic figures, along with the inscription "Memoria in Eterna." The monument is shell bronze and was fabricated by the Gorham Bronze Company in Providence, Rhode Island, at a cost of $12,000. (Photo courtesy of The Athenaeum of Philidelphia.)

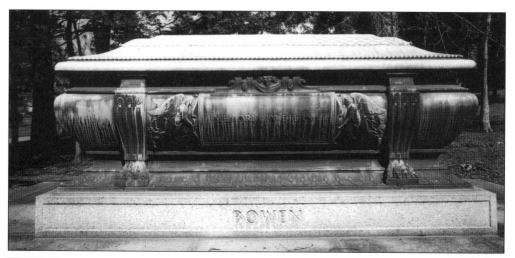

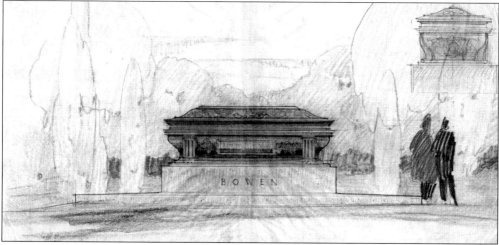

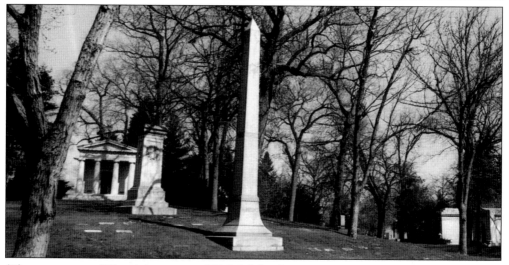

(Photo courtesy of The Athenaeum of Philidelphia.)

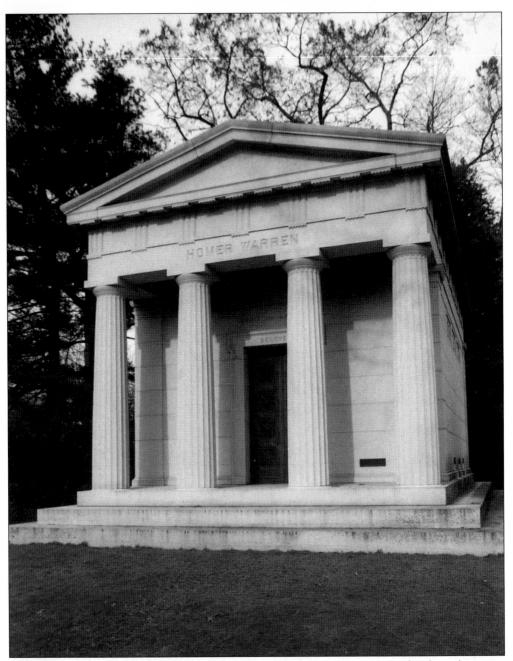

47. HOMER WARREN, 1855–1928 . Homer Warren founded the company that bears his name in 1884 and continues today. Many of Detroit's outstanding realtors were associated with Warren. He has long been recognized as the dean of Detroit real estate, as he was the first President of the Detroit Real Estate Board. Actively involved in civic affairs, he endorsed Mayor Pingree's attack on inflated street railway fares.

The design of this mausoleum is based on a Roman temple, derived from the earlier Classical Greek style, with the addition of a portico of columns on the front.

45. HENRY J. BARBER, 1879–1928. Barber was a builder and real estate dealer in the Detroit area who contributed to the development and improvement of the city.

The Barber plot is marked by a Celtic cross. The four appendages of the cross contain the signs of the four Evangelists: Matthew, the angel; Mark, the lion, Luke, the ox, and John, the eagle. Knotwork intertwines on the vertical shaft with fruitlike projections. Unfortunately, the sculptor did not leave a name for such detailed work.

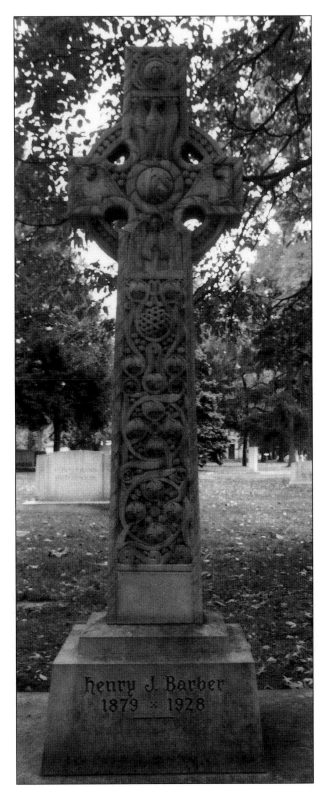

46. BENJAMIN TOBIN, 1865–1920. Identified with the automobile industry since its infancy, Tobin was President of the Continental Motors Manufacturing Company. It was one of the largest manufacturing internal combustion engines concerns in the United States. Continental's move to Detroit was initiated by an order from the Hudson Motor Car Company for 10,000 engines. Detroit went on to become the headquarters for Continental. The plant was built on East Jefferson in 1911, which was designed by Albert Kahn, not too far from the Hudson plant on East Jefferson too, and also designed by Kahn. The plant occupied 12 acres of the 30-acre site. The Continental Motor Company was a prominent factor in the industrial development of Detroit. The engines manufactured at Continental powered 100 different makes of U.S. cars, half the trucks in the country, plus many planes, boats, and agricultural vehicles. Continental ventured into automobile manufacturing (1933–34) which was short-lived.

Benjamin Tobin was one of the most widely known and respected executives in the automobile industry. Upon his death, a friend was quoted as saying, "He pushed forward the wheels of progress and Detroit stands as a greater city by reason of his activity."

The Tobin monument is in the form of a peristyle with Roman columns surrounding an interior space with seats for relatives to dwell on memories of the deceased. (Photo courtesy of Walter P. Reuther Library, Wayne State University.)

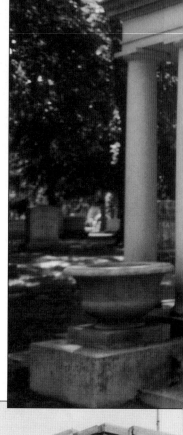

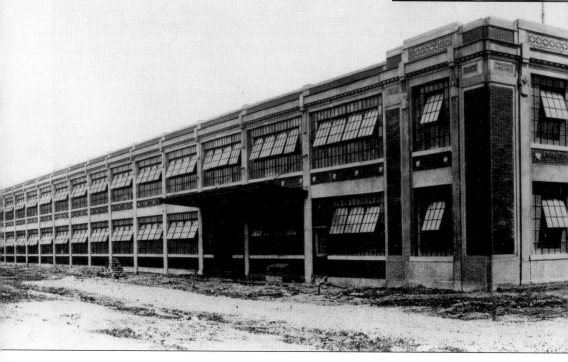

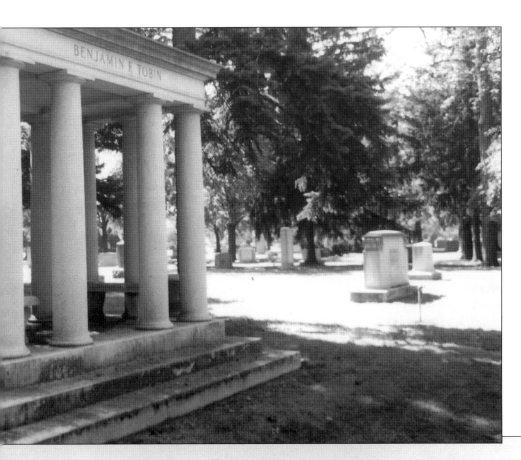

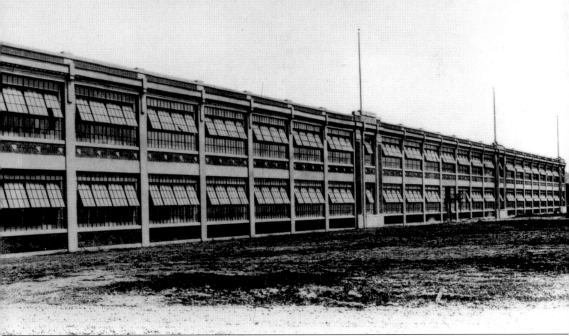

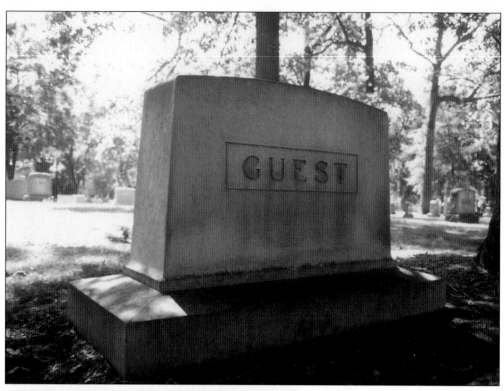

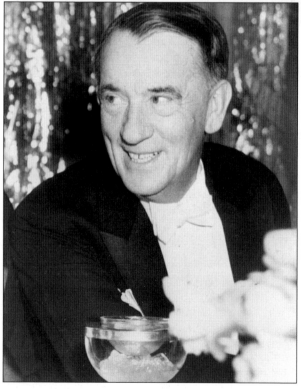

48. Edgar A. Guest, 1881–1959. Guest was referred to as "the people's poet." In 1895, the year before Henry Ford took his first ride in a motor vehicle, Eddie Guest was hired by the *Detroit Free Press* as a 13-year-old office boy. He stayed there for 60 years. He became a master of verse with metered rhyme. For more than 30 years, there was never a day that the *Free Press* went to press without Guest's verse on its pages. Perhaps his most classic verse was, "It's takes a heap o' livin' in a house t' make it home." He spoke of his ability to acquire esteem and affection by pleasing others. There was no parallel for the attachment between Guest and his public. According to his son, Bud Guest, "Dad's two great loves in life were my mother and his newspaper." (Photo courtesy of Walter P. Reuther Library, Wayne State University.)

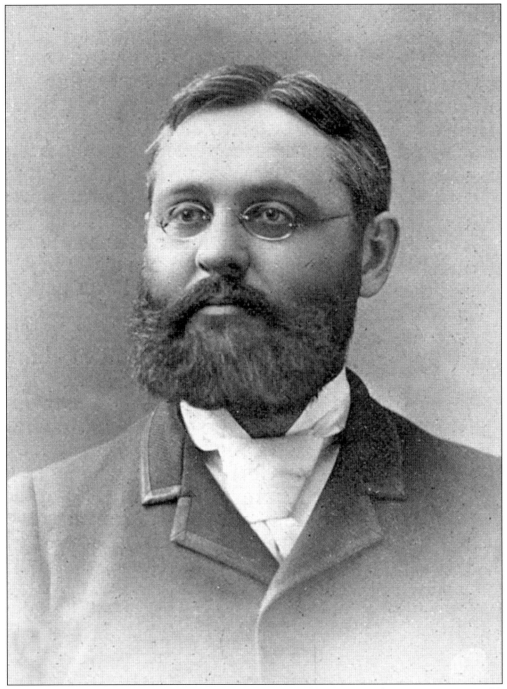

49. Allan Howard Frazer and John Palmer Frazer, 1859–1921, 1882–1972
Frazer was one of Detroit's more prominent citizens for more than a quarter of a century, having served four consecutive terms as prosecuting attorney for Wayne County (1892–1913), during which time he fought election frauds and favoritism in the prosecutor's office.

John Frazer was involved in real estate development with Frank Couzens, son of James Couzens, in the Palmer Woods section of Detroit. On his own, Frazer invested in Grosse Pointe properties.

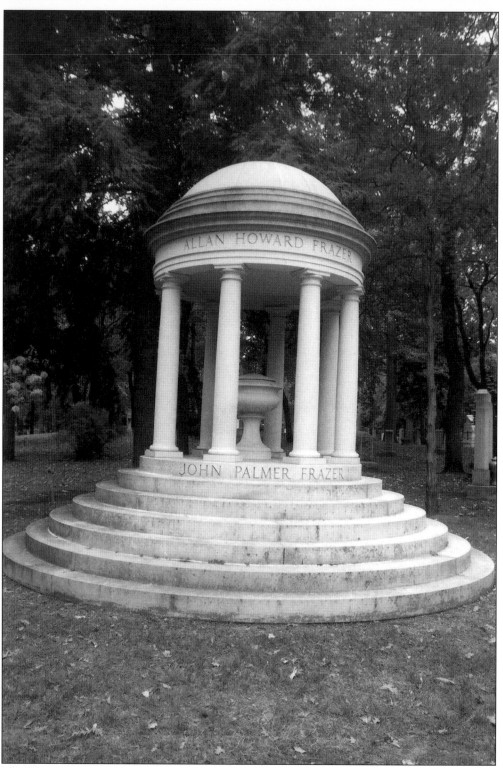

The Frazer monument is an impressive cylindrical Doric temple with a domical cap.

Five

SECTIONS 12, 23, 26, 20A, AND 21B

(PLOTS 50–55)

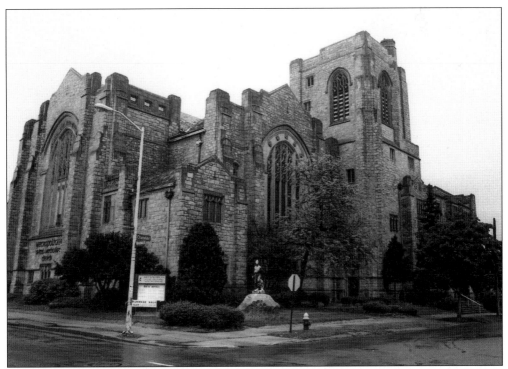

50. MERTON STACHER RICE, 1872–1943. Coined as "Preacher Mike," Rice was pastor of the Metropolitan United Methodist church in Detroit (1913–1943). One of his most ambitious undertakings was that of a fund-raiser with his golden voice that brought in $446,000 of pledges in a single day for a new church that ended up costing $1.5 million and was built in 1926. The owner of one of Detroit's tallest commercial buildings praised Rice for building a more imposing structure than his own without a mortgage. The congregation, which totaled 1,200 when Dr. Rice arrived, grew to 6,700, the largest in the Methodist faith.

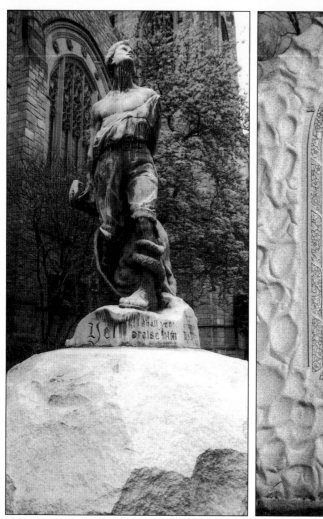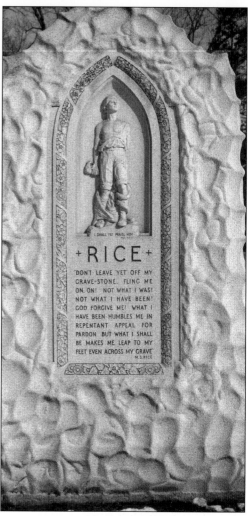

This beautiful memorial, at Woodlawn, was erected by friends of Merton Rice. It is constructed of gray granite rock, standing nine and one-half feet tall, and is ruggedly hewn, reflecting the man who it memorializes. The figure on the memorial is a reproduction of a statue in front of the church by Danish-born sculptor Alfred Nygard, who was a member of the congregation. The quotation inscribed on the face was selected by Mrs. Rice from a sermon, "Yet," which Preacher Mike once gave, reflecting his faith as a once great preacher.

51. JOSEPH BOYER, 1848–1930. Boyer was the inventor of the first successful pneumatic hammer at his machine company in St. Louis. William Burroughs rented space in Boyer's shop where he worked on the design of the adding machine he invented, which became the forerunner of today's calculator. Undoubtedly, with his own mechanical expertise, Boyer became enthused about Burroughs' efforts, which he invested in and manufactured. Burroughs then founded the American Arithmometer Company. Burroughs died in 1898, and Boyer went on to become president of the company in 1902. He moved the company to Detroit in 1905, where it became the Burroughs Adding Machine Company.

Boyer was Albert Kahn's first industrial client; the architect designed the Boyer Machine Company plant in 1901 on Second Avenue in Detroit. Boyer also recruited Kahn to design the Burroughs plant.

His son, Joseph Boyer Jr., was a famous race car driver and winner of the Indy 500 in 1924. He was considered one of the auto racing greats, although he died the same year in another car race in Pennsylvania. (Photo courtesy of Walter P. Reuther Library, Wayne State University.)

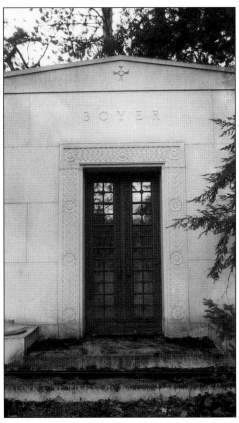

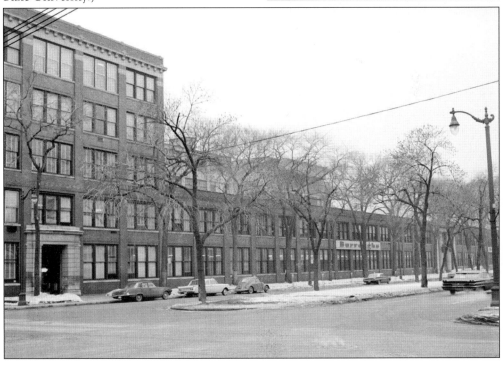

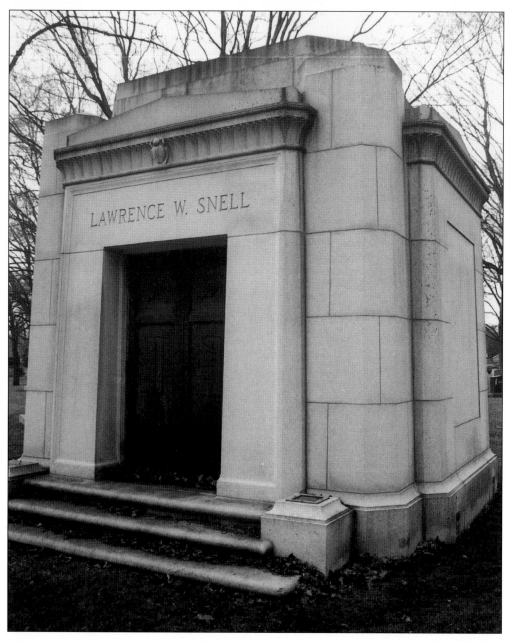

52. Lawrence W. Snell, 1870–1926. Snell was an organizer of the Highland Park State Bank with Henry Ford and James Couzens. He was state Senator of the First Disitrict in Michigan (1909–12). He invested in real estate in the north Woodward area, and owned 1,000 acres of land in what is now the city of Ferndale.

The Snell mausoleum was designed by Detroit architect Louis Kamper in 1927. It is an Egyptian Revival structure with four massive corner piers. A scarab beetle is prominently displayed over the front entrance in a concave cornice. The beetle symbolizes renewal and regeneration. It laid its eggs in a ball of dung that was rolled across the ground. This act was related by the ancient Egyptians to the sun's heavenly circuit and its daily renewal.

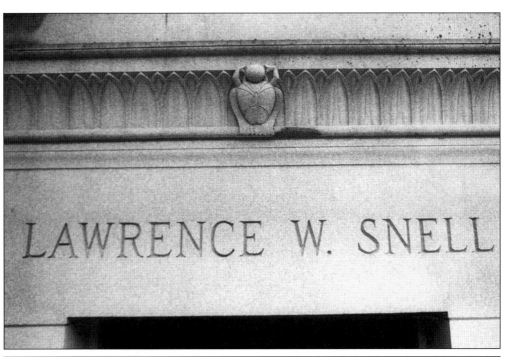

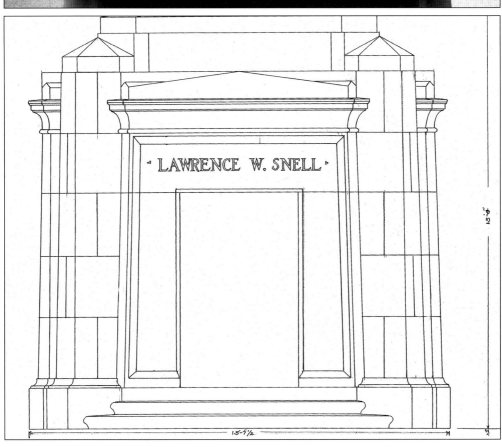

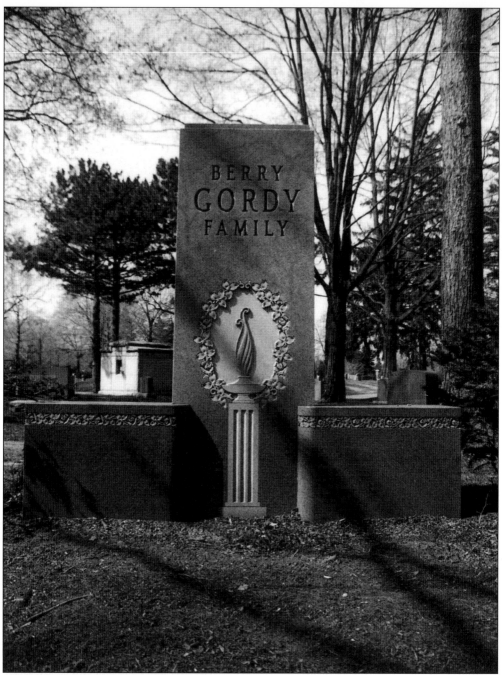

53. Berry Gordy Sr., 1888–1978. Berry Gordy Sr. was in the plastering and carpentry business, along with owning a general store and printing business. His son, Berry Gordy Jr., was heavily influenced by the ambition of his father and founded Motown Records in Detroit with an $800 loan from his family. The Gordy family believed in the philosophy of Booker T. Washington, who stressed economic independence for blacks.

The Gordy monument is polished pink granite with a foliate wreath in relief surrounding an eternal flame in loving memory of the family.

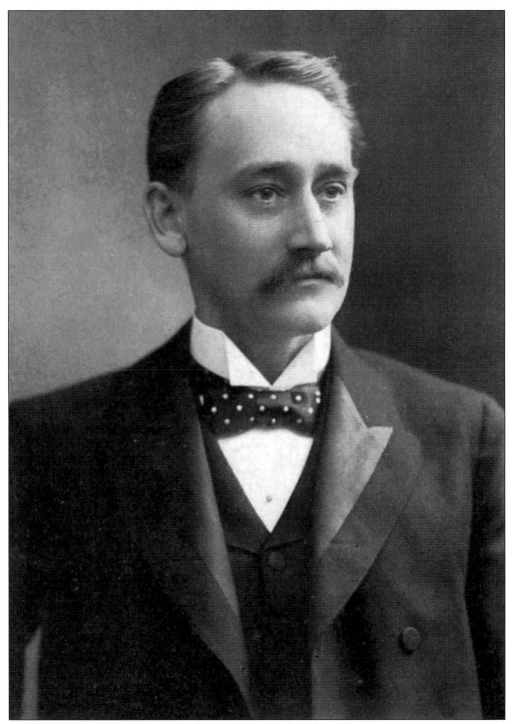

54. JOHN B. CORLISS, 1851–1929. A city attorney for Detroit (1882–86), Corliss prepared the first complete charter for Detroit which was passed by the state legislature in 1884. He went on to serve as U.S. Representative of the First District (1895–1903) after which he re-engaged in the practice of law in Detroit.

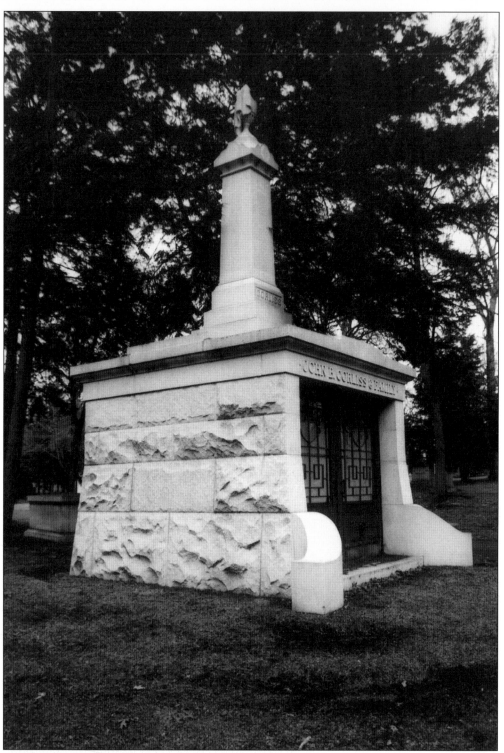

The Corliss monument is an imposing structure with a roughly hewn base, atop which is a square column with a draped urn that symbolizes the soul having fled the clothed body.

Six
SECTIONS 22, 23, 14, AND G (CHAPEL)

(PLOTS 56–62)

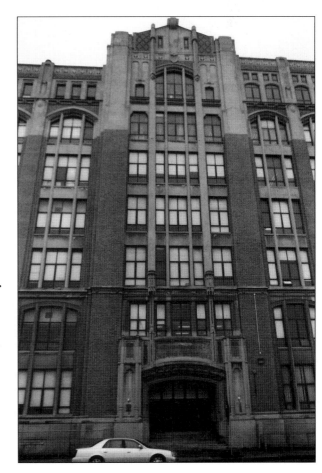

55. LUMUS NEWTON, 1854–1919. Newton was a medical doctor in Detroit. In 1900, he was elected a member of the Detroit School Board, and, during his second term, served as president. He was instrumental in starting the technical high school education program in Detroit. It led to the construction of Cass Technical High School, designed by Detroit architects Higginbotham and Malcolmson in 1917.

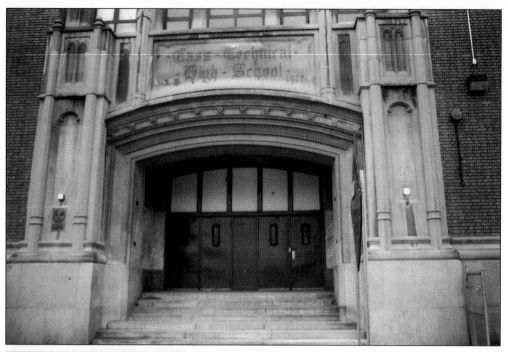

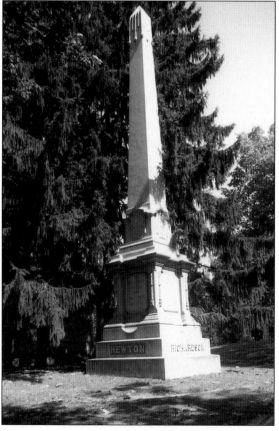

Newton's burial plot is marked by an Egyptian obelisk, a four-sided shaft with a pyramidal cap, supported by four classical style pilasters on the base. The symbol of the obelisk dates back to Egyptian antiquity and represents a ray of light or sun beam, a connection between heaven and earth. The severe proportions speak of eternal duration. The four sides of the pedestal provide room for inscriptions.

56. FRED WARDELL, 1866–1952. Fred
Wardell founded the Eureka Vacuum
Company in 1909. In 1915, Eureka was
awarded a Grand Prize by a jury of electrical
experts at the Panama Pacific International
Exposition in San Francisco. In 1919,
Wardell built a five-story company
headquarters on Broadway in downtown
Detroit. The terra cotta facade of the
building is inscribed with rich detail on the
border. By 1927, Eureka was selling one-third
of all vacuum cleaners produced in the
United States.

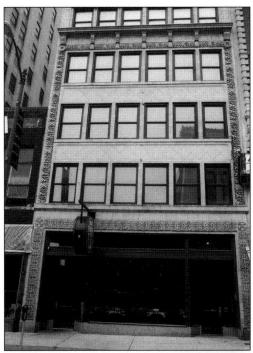

The Wardell mausoleum was created by
the Jones Brother Monument Company in
Boston. The company was once considered
the largest monument works in the world
with a granite quarry in Barre, Vermont.
They supplied granite for St. John the Divine
Cathedral in New York City. Also built of
granite, the Wardell mausoleum has a
monumental simplicity without any
historical reference.

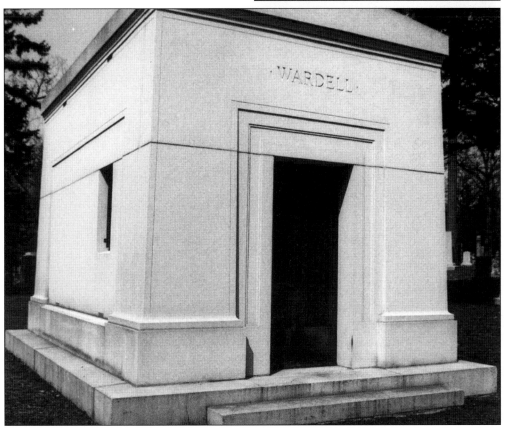

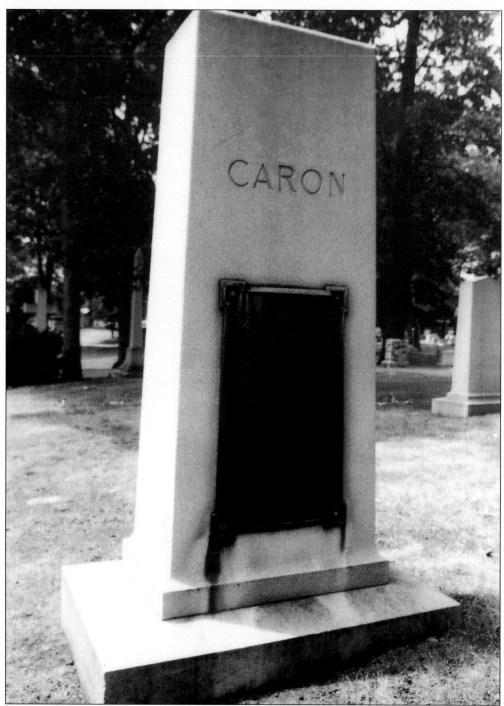

57. George Clark Caron, 1896–1916. Caron was a law student at the University of Michigan when he tragically drowned while swimming in Lake Huron. The monument is a simple tablet with a bronze plaque that contains a poem, "A Tribute to George Clark Caron," written by *Free Press* writer Edgar Guest, who was noted for his daily poetry. This monument was done by the Lloyd brothers.

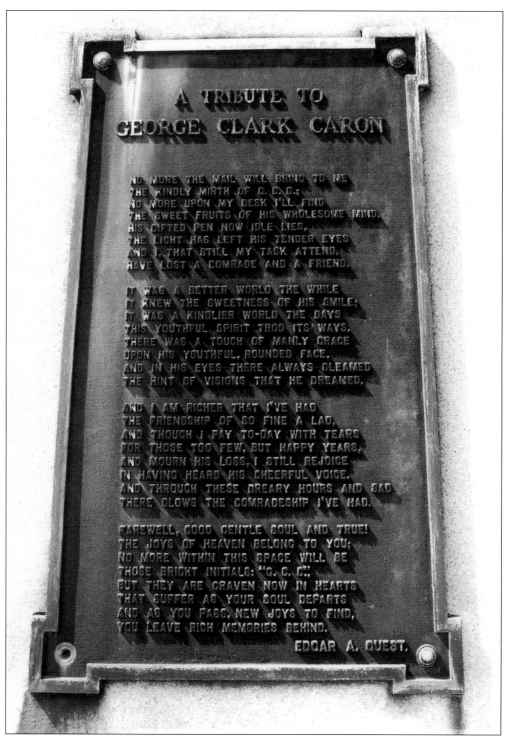

**A TRIBUTE TO
GEORGE CLARK CARON**

NO MORE THE MAIL WILL BRING TO ME
THE KINDLY MIRTH OF G. C. C.;
NO MORE UPON MY DESK I'LL FIND
THE SWEET FRUITS OF HIS WHOLESOME MIND.
HIS GIFTED PEN NOW IDLE LIES,
THE LIGHT HAS LEFT HIS TENDER EYES
AND I, THAT STILL MY TASK ATTEND,
HAVE LOST A COMRADE AND A FRIEND.

IT WAS A BETTER WORLD THE WHILE
IT KNEW THE SWEETNESS OF HIS SMILE;
IT WAS A KINDLIER WORLD THE DAYS
THIS YOUTHFUL SPIRIT TROD ITS WAYS.
THERE WAS A TOUCH OF MANLY GRACE
UPON HIS YOUTHFUL, ROUNDED FACE,
AND IN HIS EYES THERE ALWAYS GLEAMED
THE HINT OF VISIONS THAT HE DREAMED.

AND I AM RICHER THAT I'VE HAD
THE FRIENDSHIP OF SO FINE A LAD,
AND THOUGH I PAY TO-DAY WITH TEARS
FOR THOSE TOO FEW, BUT HAPPY YEARS,
AND MOURN HIS LOSS, I STILL REJOICE
IN HAVING HEARD HIS CHEERFUL VOICE.
AND THROUGH THESE DREARY HOURS AND SAD
THERE GLOWS THE COMRADESHIP I'VE HAD.

FAREWELL, GOOD GENTLE SOUL AND TRUE!
THE JOYS OF HEAVEN BELONG TO YOU;
NO MORE WITHIN THIS SPACE WILL BE
THOSE BRIGHT INITIALS: "G. C. C.,"
BUT THEY ARE GRAVEN NOW IN HEARTS
THAT SUFFER AS YOUR SOUL DEPARTS
AND AS YOU PASS, NEW JOYS TO FIND,
YOU LEAVE RICH MEMORIES BEHIND.

EDGAR A. GUEST.

Obviously touched by Guest's writing, which he read, Caron wrote to Guest expressing his views.
Somewhere along the line they met, and Guest was equally touched by Caron, revealed in this
lovely poem in which he candidly describes the young man.

121

58. EDWARD D. STAIR, 1859–1951. In 1885, Stair was owner of the Livingston Republican, one of Michigan's oldest weekly newspapers in Howell, Michigan. He also managed the opera house in Howell and used the newspaper to advertise the theater as "first class amusement." In 1886, the actress Jessie Bonstelle came to Howell to star in a play called "Gypsy Prophecy." She made an impression on Stair, who rewrote the play, called it "Trixie, the Romp Heiress," and arranged to take it on the road to New York. Jessie went on to found the Bostelle Theater in Detroit.

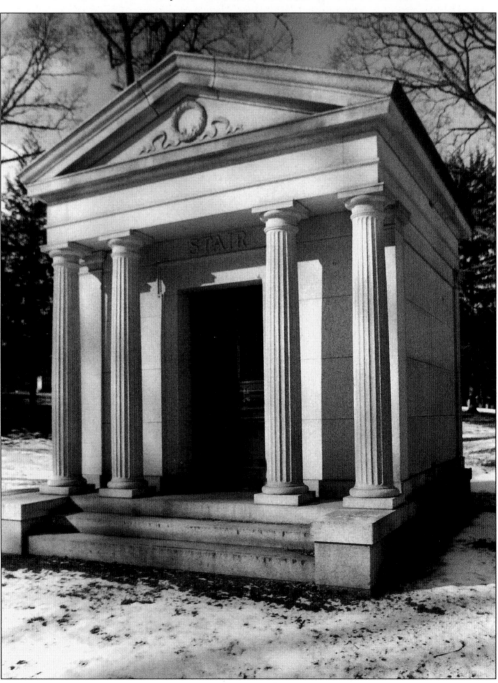

Stair got involved in the theater business. He went on to own and manage 200 theaters in the United States and Canada. In 1901, he bought his first Detroit newspaper, the *Detroit Journal.* Then, in 1917, he bought a controlling interest in the *Detroit Free Press*, of which he became the editor. In 1925, he was instrumental in hiring architect Albert Kahn to design a 14-story office building at Lafayette and Cass to house the newspaper. He invested in Detroit real estate that made him, at one time, the leading taxpayer in the city.

The Detroit Free Press was sold in 1940 to John S. Knight. Upon Stair's death in 1951, in a eulogy, Knight said: "E.D.'s lifespan covered 92 fruitful years ranging from humble beginnings as the editor of a small town weekly to great achievements in business, theatrical, banking and the publishing world. The name E.D. Stair was synonymous with rugged individualism..."

The Stair mausoleum is Greek Revival with double Doric columns flanking each side of the entry door. A wreath, commemorating victory over death, is centered in the triangular pediment. (Photo courtesy of Walter P. Reuther Library, Wayne State University.)

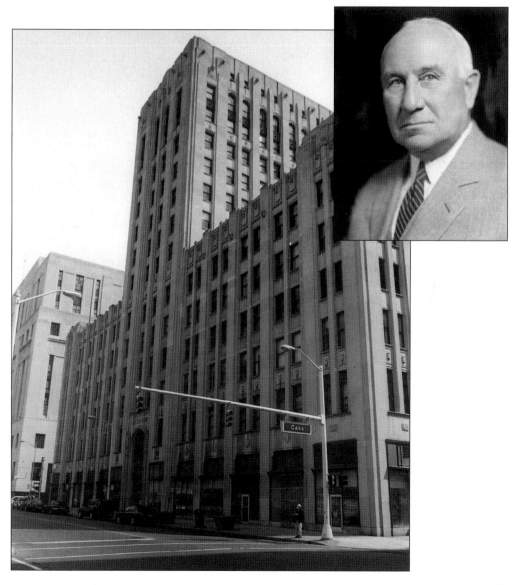

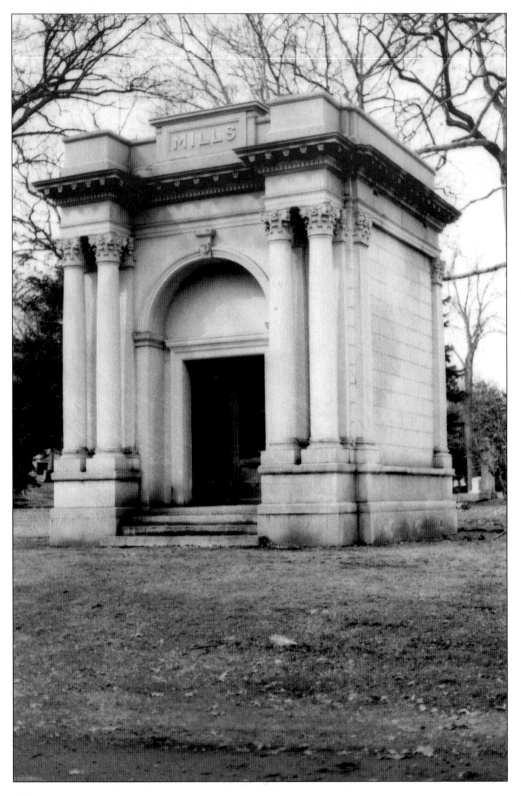

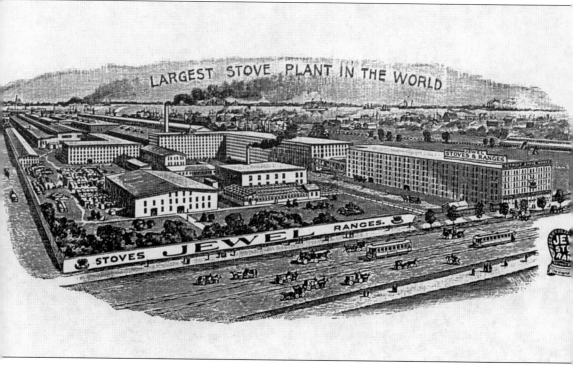

59. MERRILL I. AND MERRIL B. MILLS, 1819–1882, 1854–1929. Mills was an organizer and treasurer of the Detroit Stove Works in 1864. It boasted that it was the largest stove factory in the world and made 30,000 stoves per year. Thirteen hundred workers manufactured 80,000 to 100,000 stoves per year at the company's 10-acre site on Jefferson near Belle Isle. In 1872, Mills also invested in the Michigan Stove Company, where he became vice-president. Both firms contributed to making Detroit the stove capital of the world. The stove industry was also an important part of Detroit's early metalworking heritage that helped pave the way for the auto industry.

When the companies exhibited their wares at the Michigan State Fair in 1880, President Hayes, who attended the exhibit, referred to the stoves as "true jewels," prompted by the Detroit Stove Jewel model. Mills was elected Detroit mayor in 1866 and again in 1867, serving what were then one-year terms. He was founder of the Banner Tobacco Company in 1878 and served on the board of directors of First National Bank, which was Detroit's largest financial institution. His son, Merrill B., succeeded his father's positions with both companies. They merged in 1927, undoubtedly initiated by Merrill B.

The Mills mausoleum is designed in the French Beaux Arts style, which emphasized Classical (Greek) forms and elaborate detailing. The primary inspiration for this style was Chicago's Columbian Exposition of 1893. Monumental paired Corinthian columns flank the grand arched entry on a raised ashlar base. Corinthian pilasters mark the four corners of the building. A cornice with dentils completes the top of the building.

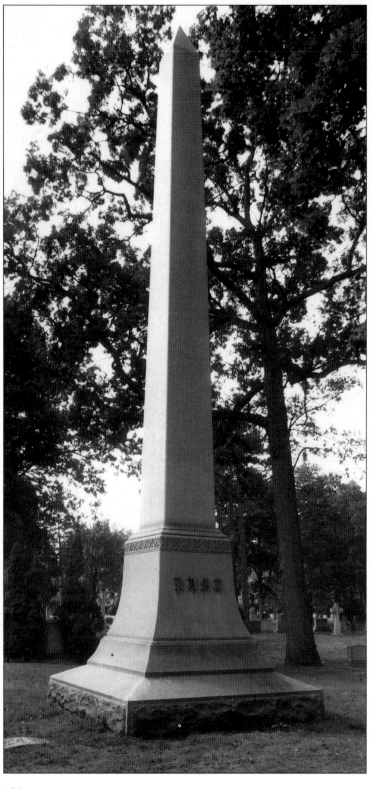

60. David W. Rust, 1873–1918. Rust was a Michigan lumberman who started out in the St. Clair County region. He then went on to become involved with the lumber trade in the Saginaw region. Together with his brothers, the Rusts were considered to have had major interests in the Michigan lumber business. This was a time when pine was king in Michigan, bringing wealth to such timber barons as David Rust.

This Egyptian obelisk, which marks the Rust family plot, is associated with ancient greatness and can be used as a monument in a relatively small space. Obelisks were less costly than the more elaborate mausoleums, yet are a distinctive marker for a grave plot. This obelisk is constructed of one continuous granite piece that measures 35 feet in height.

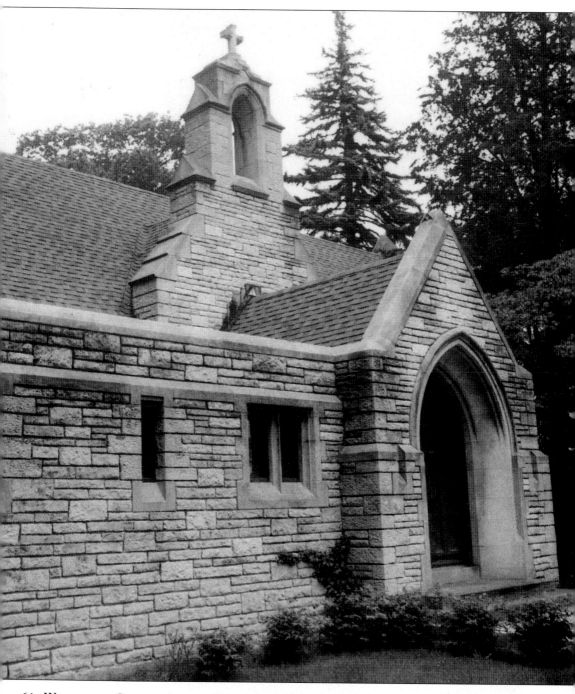

61. WOODLAWN CHAPEL, ALBERT KAHN, 1917. This building was designed by Kahn in the Gothic Revival style. He embraced historic styles for public buildings while his factory designs were more utilitarian.

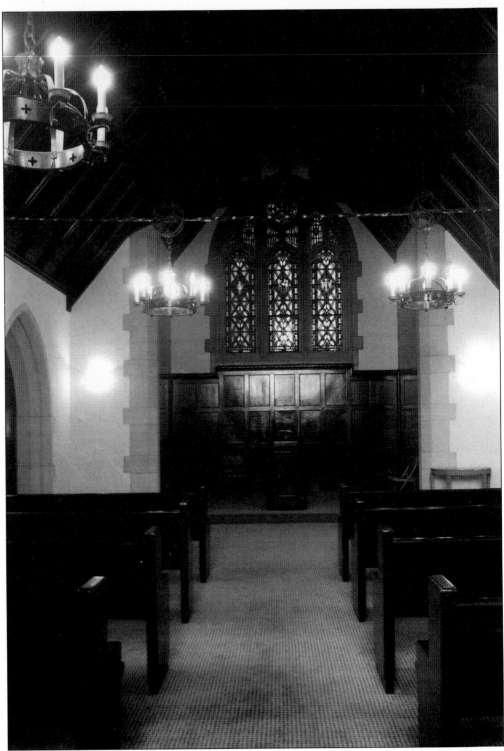

Small in scale, the interior has an intimacy and warmth with carved wooden beams overhead. The outside walls are covered with roughly hewn stonework.